FORM AND FUNCTION

Form and Function

REMARKS ON ART, DESIGN, AND
ARCHITECTURE

BY *Horatio Greenough*

EDITED BY *Harold A. Small*

WITH AN INTRODUCTION BY
Erle Loran

UNIVERSITY OF CALIFORNIA PRESS
BERKELEY, LOS ANGELES, LONDON

UNIVERSITY OF CALIFORNIA PRESS
BERKELEY AND LOS ANGELES
UNIVERSITY OF CALIFORNIA, LTD.
LONDON, ENGLAND

PRINTED IN THE UNITED STATES OF AMERICA

9 10 11 12 13 14 15

Editor's Preface

Horatio greenough *was born in Boston, September 6, 1805, one of the eleven children of a self-made man who dealt in real estate and built some of the houses in Colonnade Row. Horatio entered Harvard in 1821 and left before the end of his senior year for Italy, his diploma following after; he was determined to be a sculptor and could not begin too soon. He had encouragement from Washington Allston, and letters to Thorwaldsen in Rome. In 1829 he set up a studio in Florence, where he became, "in a manner," as his brother Henry said, "a pupil of Bartolini," an Italian portrait sculptor whose work he admired; and in the course of the next twenty-two years, most of which he spent in Florence, he produced many portrait busts on commission, also full-lengths, and several imaginative groups, single figures, and bas-reliefs: "our good folk," he was driven to complain, "think statues can be turned out like yards of sheeting." His sitters, abroad or at home, included John Quincy Adams, Lafayette, and James Fenimore Cooper. For Cooper he produced the "Chanting Cherubs," the first marble group from the chisel of an American artist. Allston wrote to Daniel Webster, recommending Greenough to execute a statue of George Washington for the Government; Cooper and Edward Everett backed the recommendation; and the result was the seated colossus, intended for the rotunda of the Capitol, which is now retired to the Smithsonian. Greenough also executed for the Capitol the group entitled "The Rescue", an American colonial settler restraining an Indian from tomahawking a woman and her infant while a large dog stands inactively by, which adorns a buttress of the steps to the East Front door. But it is not for his sculptures that Greenough is remembered; it is rather for his ideas. These are embodied in two books:* The Travels, Observations, and Experience of a Yankee Stonecutter *(New York, G. P. Putnam, 1852), in which, under the pseudonym of Horace Bender, he presented a collection of his magazine and newspaper articles, squibs, and fragments; and the* Memorial of Horatio Greenough *(New York, G. P. Putnam, 1853) issued soon after the sculptor's death—he died at Somerville December 18, 1852—by Henry T. Tuckerman, the art critic. Much of the* Travels *is repeated, verbatim or with slight modifications, in the* Memorial, *but the present book is based on Tuckerman's* because it includes three good pieces which are not in Greenough's own. Of the twelve pieces selected by Tuckerman, four are here omitted as contributing little to the main theme. A few printer's errors in the Memorial, and a few antique spellings and stylistic particulars, have been silently corrected or altered; the punctuation has been made easier; and some notes have been added, which are enclosed in square brackets to distinguish them from Greenough's. Otherwise, the present edition faithfully renews a good work that has been too long neglected.

That Greenough has enduring value and interest is indicated by the fact that a modern American painter and teacher of painting supplies our Introduction. He speaks strongly for Greenough's creative ideals. He does not omit to say that Greenough's sculptures are less than admirable, nor that his ideas about painting are outmoded. (One must remember that the notion of painting as mere copying was as old as Aristotle, and rare indeed the artist who heeded Plato's passing remark that paintings could be imitations of Truth.) But Mr. Loran finds that Greenough reads, in the main, like a progressive contemporary. That is intended to be the emphasis of the book.

H. A. S.

Contents

Introduction, by Erle Loran

THE CREATIVE IDEAL THAT "form follows function" is now commonly associated with architects like Frank Lloyd Wright. We trace Wright's development back to Sullivan and thence to Richardson, who was born in 1838. To most, it will come as a surprise to learn that the American sculptor, Horatio Greenough, born in 1805, had formulated ideas on art and architecture that read, even today, like the words of a progressive contemporary.

The primitive setting of art in America in Greenough's time is portrayed in the first essay, "Aesthetics at Washington." We find him pleading for the establishment of the first school of design in America! "I believe that these States need art as a visible exponent of their civilization." Greenough is well aware of the obstacles standing in the way, and he recalls that "the first work of sculpture by an American hand exhibited in this country, executed for the illustrious [James Fenimore] Cooper, was a group of children. The artist [Greenough himself] was rebuked and mortified by loud complaints of their nudity." Perhaps, because he is afraid of aiming too high, he does not ask for a school of fine arts. Instead, he modestly says, "I desire to see working normal schools of structure and ornament, constantly occupied in designing for the manufacturers, and for all mechanics who need aesthetical guidance in their operations." This program is not unlike that of the pre-Nazi German Bauhaus. He thus addresses himself to the practical, business-minded American, arguing that only when American goods are designed with distinction will they be able to compete with English and French importations.

He proceeds immediately to a severe criticism of the lack of *functionalism* in the building and landscape architecture in Washington. Criticizing the high-relief sculpture in the tympanum of the Capitol building, he says, "it is the translation of rhetoric into stone— a feat often fatal to the rhetoric, always fatal to the stone."

With words that might be spoken by a contemporary and progressive architect he outlines the requirements of important public "edifices." In terms of function the rule must be "to plant a building firmly on the ground," that is, to adapt its size and form to the terrain (site); "the monumental character of a building has reference to its site—to its adaptation in size and form to that site. It has reference also to the *external expression* of the *inward functions* of the building." The most advanced modern architects could aspire to no higher ideal.

In answer to the question whether Greek art should be imitated his answers are timely and pertinent, for this, alas, is no dead issue, as we can see by looking around us on campuses and business streets. To clarify his point of view he turns to problems of locomotion, then so timely. He says, "I contend for Greek principles, not Greek things. If a flat sail goes nearest wind, a bellying sail, though picturesque, must be given up. The men who have reduced locomotion to its simplest elements, in the trotting wagon and the yacht *America,* are nearer to Athens at this moment than they who would bend the Greek temple to every use." The inevitable result of such misguided designing "is a make-believe. It is not the real thing. We see the marble capitals; we trace the acanthus leaves of a celebrated model—incredulous; it is not a temple." And again, in words that belong to this very moment, "let us *encourage experiment* at the risk of license, rather than submit to an iron rule that begins by sacrificing reason, dignity, and comfort."

Greenough offers practical guidance for his program of functionalism. He says, "let us consult nature—in our search after the great principles of construction." In the animal world "there is no arbitrary law of proportion, no unbending model of form. There is scarce a part of the animal organization which we do not find elongated or shortened, increased, diminished, or suppressed, as the wants of the genus or species dictate, as their exposure or their work may require." The logic and rightness is found in the "consistency and harmony of the parts juxtaposed, the *subordination of details to masses,* and of masses to the whole. *The law of adaptation is the fundamental law of nature in all structure."*

Therefore, in designing architecture, "instead of forcing the functions of every sort of building into one general form, without reference to the inner distribution, let us begin from the heart as a nucleus, and *work outward"*—"the unflinching adaptation of a building to its position and use gives, as a sure product of that adaptation, character and expression." In contemporary words, "form follows function." As Greenough admires the flawless functionalism observed in nature, he also praises the American construction of ships, machines, and bridges. He is unsparing in his ridicule of those who would mask bad architecture with the "sneaking copy of a Greek façade." An inappropriate and borrowed architectural style produces an effect similar to the "African king, standing in mock majesty with his legs and feet bare, and his body clothed in a cast coat of the Prince Regent." Mr. Thomas Jefferson, who "recommends the model of the Maison Carrée for the State House at Richmond," is consequently not praised for his suggestion. Greenough wanted America to invent her own forms, to suit her own climate and needs.

Greenough is always aware of the distinction between purely monumental structures "addressed to the sympathies, the faith, or the taste of a people" and those more practical structures that "may be classed as organic, formed to meet the wants of their occupants." In buildings of the latter group "the laws of structure and apportionment, depending on definite wants, obey a demonstrable rule. *They may be called machines.*" And this was not Le Corbusier talking in 1930, but

Greenough before 1850! In the essay, "Relative and
Independent Beauty," Greenough has a good deal to
say about meaningless decoration, the curse of architecture in many lands and times. In French, *chinoiserie*
means tomfoolery as well as elaborate Chinese decoration. In American architecture, "gingerbread" has
come to mean something like excrescence, to be removed like a cancer. But Greenough could see its false-
ness while it was having its heyday. He speaks of
"embellishment as false beauty"—"the instinctive effort
of infant civilization to disguise its incompleteness,
even as God's completeness is to infant science disguised." Whitman was hardly more than borrowing
from Greenough when he wrote in the preface to
Leaves of Grass (1855): "In paintings or mouldings or
carvings in mineral or wood . . . , or to put upon cor-
nices or monuments . . . or to put anywhere before the
human eye indoors or out, that which distorts honest
shapes . . . is a nuisance and revolt. . . . Of ornaments
to a work nothing outré can be allowed—but those
ornaments can be allowed that conform to the perfect
facts of the open air and that flow out of the nature of
the work and come irrepressibly from it and are necessary to the completion of the work. Most works are
most beautiful without ornament."

To the modern artist and architect, function and organization are either synonyms or firmly interlaced concepts. Now, beauty is a word sparingly used by modern creative men, but Greenough has a definition that is very easy to take: "Beauty is the promise of Function." Similarly, God is a concept that modern men usually try to express in some indirect way, but when Greenough speaks of the existence of "one truth, even as there is one God, and that organization is his utterance" we can at least transpose his meaning without difficulty. "Now, organization obeys his law. It obeys his law by an approximation to the essential, and then there is what we term life; or it obeys his law by falling short of the essential, and then there is disorganization. I have not seen the inorganic attached to the organized but as a symptom of imperfect plan, or of impeded function, or of extinct action."

"The normal development of beauty is through action to completeness. The invariable development of embellishment and decoration is more embellishment and more decoration. The *reductio ad absurdum* is palpable enough at last; but where was the first downward step? I maintain that the first downward step was *the introduction of the first inorganic, nonfunctional element, whether of shape or color*"—"the aim of the artist, therefore, should be first to seek the essential"—"the essential will be complete."

Greenough refers to the shape, color, and markings of animals and birds with sublime confidence that in God's world there is no meaningless embellishment, no decoration for its own sake. It remained for another American, the painter Abbott Thayer, to publish in 1907 the first treatise on animal markings as concealment. (Adaptive coloration and concealment in animals form the basis for the modern approach to camouflage in warfare.) Thus purpose and function are seen as law in animal forms and man is urged to achieve harmony with that law in his own creations. Organization through function must be the guiding rule in art and architecture. "God's world has a distinct formula for every function, and we shall seek in vain to borrow shapes; we must make the shapes, and can only effect this by mastering the principles."

Not every page in these essays will be equally rewarding. Occasional quaintnesses of expression and obscurity in the presentation of ideas mar the generally valuable material in hand. Nor is the reader urged to look up the sculpture produced by Greenough, even though it is an unaffected, straightforward product. His ideas on painting are likewise uninteresting. But it is of great historical interest to discover that an early American artist of repute in his own day was not in agreement with practices that might otherwise appear to have been accepted without question. He even dared to put Thomas Jefferson's ideas on architecture in an unfavorable light. It is reassuring also to know that such an artist showed the same appreciation of truly native American forms that the sophisticated in our day admire for their directness and simplicity. We know these forms now—notably the furniture—as "Early American." The lesson of Greenough has yet to be learned, especially by many architects who still hold power. What a bitter pill it should be for them to know that they are at least a hundred years behind the times, by standards set up by one of our own good ancestors in America! Instead of putting up resistance to the innovations of the European International School, with its "machines for living," and to the boldness and rashness of Frank Lloyd Wright, they might all this time have turned their fury against the farseeing Horatio Greenough.

Aesthetics at Washington

AN AMERICAN citizen who has gone abroad to study a refined art presents himself before his fellow countrymen at disadvantage. To the uninitiated his very departure from these shores is an accusation of the fatherland. If he sail away to strike the whale on the Pacific, or load his hold with the precious teeth, and gums, and sands of Africa, it is well; but to live for years among Italians, Frenchmen, and Germans, for the sake of breathing the air of high art, ancient and modern, this is shrewdly thought by many to show a lack of genius, whose boast it is to create, and we are often asked triumphantly if nature is not to be found here on this continent. They who thus reason and thus feel are not aware of the peculiar position of the aspirant to artistic activity in these States. They see that lawyers and statesmen, divines, physicians, mechanics, all are here developed, are said to be home-grown, nay, often also self-made. They forget that all the elements of our civilization have been imported. They forget that our schools and colleges, our libraries and churches, are filled with the most material proof that Greek and Roman thought is even now modifying and guiding our intellectual development. A moment's attention will enable them to perceive that the American student of art only seeks to effect for his own department of knowledge a like transfer of rudimental science and, at this late day, make the form of our culture harmonious with its essential and distinctive character.

We are still imbued, deeply imbued, with the stern disregard of everything not materially indispensable which was generated by ages of colonial, and border, and semisavage life. We have imported writings on art in abundance, and there is scarcely a scholar in the land who cannot wield the terms of dilettantism as glibly as a European professor; but unfortunately for us the appreciation of an aesthetical theory without substantial art is as difficult as to follow a geometric demonstration without a diagram. It is sterile and impotent, as is all faith without works.

If the arts of design could have simply remained in a negative state, like seeds buried in autumn, to await the action of a more genial season, we should be justified in postponing even now their cultivation. But like the *Bourgeois gentilhomme,* who talked prose from his boyhood without being aware of it, we have been compelled both to design and to adorn, and our efforts, from their nature, must remain monuments of chaotic disorder in all that relates to aesthetics. In a word, we have negative quantities to deal with before we can rise to zero. I do not mean to say that the beautiful has not been sought and found amongst us. I wish, and I hope to show, that we have done more, in a right direction, than has been appreciated; much in a wrong direction, that must be examined and repudiated.

I am sensible of the disadvantage under which I labor in speaking of matters to which I have devoted my attention for many years. I regret that I have no such right to sympathy and to support as that set forth by the author of a recent work when he says, "I have no qualifications for a critic in art, and make no pretensions to the character. I write only for the great multitude, as ill instructed in this sphere as I cheerfully admit myself." When the writer of that profession shall have learned what the main qualifications for a critic on art really are, I cannot believe that he will cheerfully renounce them; and far as I am from a personal acquaintance with the great multitude, I cannot believe that one "as ill instructed as themselves" is the exact person whom they would depute to deal with matters which, to say the least of them, require some training.

It is the great multitude that has decided the rank of the statesmen, the poets, and the artists of the world. It is the great multitude for whom all really great things are done, and said, and suffered. The great multitude desires the best of everything, and in the long run is the best judge of it. I have said this much in relation to the aesthetical observations of this writer because, though I generally sympathize with his views and often admire the expression of them, I look upon the ground he here takes as one too often taken—in itself untenable, and apt to mislead by an exaggerated expression of modesty. Substantially, it is analogous to the conduct of one who should commence by declaring that all men are free and equal, and go on to give orders to the right and left as to valets. Fain would I also lay claim to the title of self-made man; indeed, I graduated at Harvard, in 182–, which they who knew the school will allow was near enough self-making to satisfy any reasonable ambition. But since then I have been indebted to very many for light as for assistance.

If there were in our character or in our institutions aught that is at war with art in the abstract, I for one would be silent, preferring the humblest labor, if any labor deserve the name of humble, to the development of an influence adverse to American freedom. I speak of art now because I think I see that it is a want—a want widely felt, deeply felt—an intellectual want, a social want, an economical want—and that to a degree which few seem to suspect. I believe that these States need art as a visible exponent of their civilization.[1]

[1] In the speech of Mr. Smith, of Alabama, in explanation of a resolution offered by him in relation to Kossuth, I find the following passage: "I will make another observation, and that is in reference to the idea of establishing republican governments in Europe. New governments there are constantly rising and falling, and they have been trying to establish republican governments for the last thousand years; have they ever succeeded? and why not? Because of their antiquities and their monuments, breathing, smacking, and smelling of nobility and royalty, and because half of the people are magnates."

I take note of this remark because I believe there is good solid truth in it. "Quoi, si je pourrai friponner quelque chose pour étayer mon pauvre petit livre!" [Cf. Montaigne, *Essais,* II, xviii.] I should have placed the magnates first in the list of obstacles to republican progress, but I will not quarrel about precedence. The statesmen may be allowed to settle this matter.

I rejoice to find that American legislators have found out the value and significance of monuments, and of antiquities in their political influence. May we not expect that our civilization and our institutions will obtain this support from Congress? I hope, in a subsequent paper, to urge this matter more fully. I will now merely state that there stands in the studio of Mr. Powers, at Florence, a statue of America which is not only a beautiful work of art but which "breathes, smacks, and smells" of republicanism and Union. If placed conspicuously, by Mr. Walter, in one of the new wings of the Capitol, it would be a monument of Union. The sooner it is done, the sooner it will become an "antiquity." [Hiram Powers' statue, "America," hopefully intended

They call for it as a salvation from merely material luxury and sensual enjoyment, they require it as the guide and ornament of inevitable structure and manufacture.

Joyfully have the governing men of England, France, and Germany beheld in the United States that policy which has denied all national education except for the purpose of war and trade. Joyfully have they seen the individual States equally blind to the swift-coming requirements of this people; and they have founded and perfected schools of design, of which the abler pupils are employed in illustrating the national history; the lower talents fill the factory, the foundry, and the atelier, to fashion fabrics for ourselves. From Boston to New Orleans no house, no tavern, no bar-room, I had almost said, that does not give proof, by the tawdry spawn of European manufacture, of our tribute to their *savoir faire* and their appreciation of our taste. But what, it will be asked, has the development of art to do with manufactures? High art stands, in relation to manufactures and all the so-called lower trades, where high literature stands in relation to social

as an ornament to the National Capitol—perhaps to crown its dome,—was destroyed by fire in a Brooklyn warehouse in 1866. Thomas U. Walter was the architect for the extension of the Capitol. He designed the wings and dome, added in 1851–1865.]

and to civil life. Ask how much of the fruit of high culture and mental training reaches the public through the forum, the pulpit, and the diurnal press, and you will have the measure of the influence of pure art on structure and manufacture in all their branches. Who in England urged this matter upon the attention of Parliament until the best models of Greece and Italy were placed within reach of every manufacturing population? The Board of Trade. That body caused to be translated from foreign languages, and illustrated by elaborate drawings, the most approved works of Munich, Berlin, and Paris. They have ransacked, at great cost, the medieval magnificence of Italy to find new forms and add a grace to the products of their looms, their potteries, and their foundries. Does any statesman fancy that these governments have been invaded by a sudden love of the sublime and beautiful? I believe that they who watch our markets and our remittances will agree with me that their object is to keep the national mints of America at work for themselves; and that the beautiful must, to some extent, be cultivated here, if we would avoid a chronic and sometimes an acute tightness of the money market. The statistics of our annual importation of wares which owe their preference solely to design will throw a light on this question that will command the attention of the most thrifty and parsimonious of our legislators.

In founding a school of art we have an obstacle to surmount, viz., a puritanical intolerance thereof. The first work of sculpture by an American hand exhibited in this country, executed for the illustrious Cooper, was a group of children.[2] The artist was rebuked and mortified by loud complaints of their nudity. Those infantine forms roused an outcry of censure which seemed to have exhausted the source whence it sprang, since all the harlot dancers who have found an El Dorado in these Atlantic cities have failed to reawaken it. I say seemed to have exhausted it; but only seemed, for the same purblind squeamishness which gazed without alarm at the lascivious fandango awoke with a roar at the colossal nakedness of Washington's manly breast.[3] This fact will show how easy it is to condemn what is intrinsically pure and innocent, to say the least; how difficult to repress what is clearly bad and vicious. They who speculate upon the corrupt tastes of a public, when they have learned that genteel comedy is neglected, that tragedy is unattractive, that galleries of painting and statuary are unknown in a large and

[2] [Greenough's "Chanting Cherubs," shown in Boston in 1831. Some of the newspapers suggested that the cherubs should be draped.]

[3] [Greenough's half-nude "Washington" also offended the Grundys.]

wealthy community, such speculators take their baya-
deres thither as to a sure market. They know that a
certain duration of abstinence, voluntary or forced,
makes garbage tolerable, and ditch water a luxury. I do
not venture to hope that even high art will abolish
"cakes and ale," but I trust before many years are
elapsed no *usée* terpsichore of Paris or Vienna will be
able to show half a million as a measure of our appetite
for the meretricious.[4]

I wish not to be misunderstood for a moment as recommending a Smithsonian school, with a hierarchy of
dignitaries in art. I have elsewhere stated my conviction that such a system is hostile to artistic progress.
I desire to see working normal schools of structure and
ornament, organized simply but effectively, and constantly occupied in designing for the manufacturers,
and for all mechanics who need aesthetical guidance
in their operations—schools where emulation shall be
kindled by well-considered stimuli, and where all that
is vitally important in building or ornament shall be
thoroughly taught and constantly practiced. I know
not how far the limit of Congressional action may

[4] [In this paragraph the references to a dancer are probably to Lola Montez,
whose cavortings were the sensation of the day and highly profitable to her.
In Greenough's *Travels*, the concluding words of the paragraph are "appetite
for 'ginger.'"]

admit the founding of such schools by the central government. Should it be impossible to interest Congress in the matter, I am not without hope that some, at least, of the State legislatures may effect it; and, failing this resource, I hope that associated individuals will combine for this object. I cannot but believe that a report, called for by Congress, on the amount of goods imported which owe the favor they find here to design, would show the importance of such schools in an economical point of view. I believe that such a report would show that the schools which we refuse to support here, we support abroad, and that we are heavily taxed for them.

It surely cannot be asking too much that the seat of Government, where the national structures rise, and are yearly increasing in number and importance, should present a specimen of what the country can afford in material and workmanship, in design and ornament. If this were resolved on, a stimulus would be given to exertion, while the constant experience here acquired would soon perfect a school of architectural design.

The defects of the stone of which the Capitol was built could have been no secret to Mr. Bulfinch.[5] Had

---

[5] [Charles Bulfinch was one of the architects of the Capitol.]

there existed a board, or a school, or any other respon-
sible depository of architectural experience, we should
not have witnessed the deplorable recurrence to the
same quarries for the construction of the Patent Office
and the Treasury buildings. The outlay in paint alone,
to which recourse has been had in order to sheathe this
friable material, would have maintained a school which
would have saved us from the blunder, not to mention
the great advantage we should have derived from its
designs and its pupils. Had the amount expended in
white lead been invested, a fund would have now accumulated sufficient to reface them all with marble.
I am convinced that true economy would at this moment order the Potomac stone, wherever it has been
used, to be immediately replaced by a better material.

Setting aside, however, the question of economy,
and looking at the question of propriety, can anything
be more absurd than to expend millions upon noble
pieces of masonry, and then to smear them with lead,
thereby reducing them to a level with the meanest
shingle palace? Stone among building materials, standing where gold stands among metals, to paint stone is
like covering gold with tin foil. So far has this been
carried that even in the rotunda, where no conceivable
motive could exist for the vandalism, the entire ma-

sonry has been painted, and that too of various tints, so that I will venture to affirm that many carry away the idea that the whole is but a piece of carpenter's work. The treatment of the Treasury buildings, where the granite basement has been painted of one color, the columns of a second, and the wall behind them of a third, where even the lampposts have been daubed with divers tints, like a barber's pole, is noticed with priceless naïveté in an important public document as a *neat* piece of work. What shall we say of the balustrades, where massive iron bars have been driven bodily into the columns as though a column in a first-class building might be treated like a blind wall in the basest structure, and that, too, without a shadow of need? What shall we say of the iron railings that obtrude upon the eye about the blockings of the Patent Office, and veil, with their inharmonious blackness, the organization of that building? What of the one slender chimney of red brick which peers over the broken profile of the marble Post Office? Will any adept in the science of construction explain why the gaslight which is seen at the eastern entrance of the Capitol was made to hang with so many feet of tiny pipe, and then secured by shabby wires driven into the columns? Would any person conversant with the proprieties of building tolerate such a slovenly arrangement in a private house,—or in a private stable, if columns formed a feature of that stable? Do not such absurd and ignorant malpractices look as if a barbarous race had undertaken to enjoy the magnificence of a conquered people, and not known how to set about it? Does anyone fancy that the uninstructed multitude does not feel these incongruities? It is not so. As well may you hope to sin against grammar in your speeches, and against decency and self-respect in your dress or deportment, and expect that it will pass unobserved.

The effect produced by the grounds and shrubbery in the neighborhood of the Capitol deserves a moment's attention. There is somewhat in flowerbeds and fancy gardening, with corbeilles of ephemeral plants, so out of all keeping with the character and functions of this edifice as to give the spectator a painful sense that the idea of the adaptation of grounds to buildings has never recurred to those whose duty it was to look after these matters. Trees and verdure are beautiful, and flowers still more so, but they are impertinent adjuncts to the Capitol of the United States, and where they veil and obstruct the view of the façade, as at the Post Office, are insufferable. The creeping vines that have been led over the arches which support the platform in rear of the Naval Monument are a grosser instance of misguided search after the picturesque. If these arches are properly constructed, the vines are impertinent, for they hide their articulation. Whether well or ill built, the proximity of these vines is a destructive element, uselessly added to the inevitable wear of the weather. Further, if the principle which guided their introduction here be a sound one, logical sequence and harmony call for their appearance in other like situations.

The recent appointment of a gentleman of approved taste to superintend the arrangement of the public grounds gives well-founded reasons to hope that these, and the like unsightly anomalies, will disappear; and that all, at least within his department, will be made in harmony with the character and purposes of the chief edifice of the country.

The position of the group of Columbus and the Indian girl is anomalous and absurd; anomalous, because it invades the front view of the portico, chokes the façade, and hides another statue by the same artist; absurd, because it treats the building as somewhat on which to mount into conspicuous view, not as a noble and important vase which it is called humbly to adorn and illustrate. The statue of Washington is surrounded by dwarf cypress and clumps of rosebush. These are impertinent and ridiculous—impertinent because they hide the pedestal and obstruct the view of the inscription, thus overlaying the intention of the monument, and that for the mere display of ephemeral vegetation, a phenomenon, however attractive, not here in place— ridiculous, because they seem as if intended in some way to help and eke out the sculpture; which, when a statue of this class requires it, must be done by replacing it with something worthy to stand alone. The grass within the railing, if cut close, destroys the monumental effect by the exhibition of frequent care; if neglected, offends by its rank growth and decay. The railings which have been placed about the statues of the Capitol accuse a want of respect for the public property. They accuse it without remedying it; for in spite of their protection, perhaps because of it, the statues of Columbus and of Washington have received more injury in the few years that they have been so guarded than many figures wrought before the birth of Christ have suffered in coming to us through the so-called Dark Ages. I have several times seen boys at play on the portico of the Capitol; which, if right, makes it wrong there to place costly sculptures. If I protest against iron railings around statuary, it is because I believe they avail not for their object. I trust to the intelligence of the many to do justice to the artistic efforts made for their sake. In the end, I believe the people will be the best guardians of public works here, as they have proved themselves elsewhere. Four lamps have been placed around the statue of Washington; by night they light only the feet of the figure, by day they exactly obstruct two of the principal views of it. I doubt not that the person who so placed these lights meant to do the statue a service. He probably never heard of "the eight views" of a statue. These ever-jarring principles of magnificence and economy—laying out millions for dignity, and denying the thousands necessary to insure care, intelligence, and taste in their conservation and exposition—produce a certain compound of pretension and meanness of effect highly to be deprecated in great public works. I say highly to be deprecated, for, however they who have given no attention to art and its influences may be surprised at the assertion, such a chaos cannot be daily seen with impunity. What at first shocked soon becomes familiar, and the susceptibility to healthy impressions from the display of order, harmony, logical dependence, and adaptation are weakened if not destroyed in the observer.

I have mentioned some flagrant instances of the want of care or of knowledge on the part of those to whom the national buildings have been entrusted. This strain of remark might be continued until we had passed in review almost every detail of the structure and ornaments of the public works. It is an ungrateful task. Enough has been said to show that the evident intention of Congress to render these buildings and grounds worthy of the Nation, both in their construction and maintenance, has thus far been very imperfectly effected. I will now state what I believe to be the reason why so much outlay has produced so unsatisfactory a result. First: I believe that the absence of any clear and distinct ideas of what is becoming, dignified, and proper in the premises lies at the root of the evil. For this no one is to blame. The wants of this people have called—imperatively called—the active and able men of the country to pursuits far removed from an investigation of the beautiful, either in theory or in practice. These minds have been engaged in laying the foundations, broad and deep, of a mighty empire. They have reared the walls—they have distributed the blessed light and blessing air throughout the vast structure. They have tamed the forest, subdued the wilderness, and spread the benign influence of the gospel and of education from the Atlantic to the Pacific ocean. They have left to later days and men of other mold the task of throwing around the pillars of the State the garlands of a fine artistic culture. Had they been men intent upon the questions that occupy us now, they had been as unfit for the task imposed on them as the land was unprepared for their labors. But untutored as they were in the mysteries of art, an instinct, great, noble, and unerring, guided their decision in respect to the visible attributes of this metropolis. The selection of this site, the ground plan of this city, show the outline of a master; and years must elapse ere any school which we can found will be capable of worthily filling it. Secondly: I believe that the heterogeneous and chaotic character of these buildings and grounds arises from an ill-judged interference with technical design and arrangement on the part of men in authority, whether in the legislative or executive branches of government. Since our institutions carry with them as a necessary consequence a frequent change in the personnel of government, it is clear that if each succeeding wave of deputed authority is to leave the impress of its taste and its will upon the public structures, these must ere long be but a patchwork of as many whims, fancies, and artistic dogmas as have found favor in the eyes of the temporary occupants of place, unless some standard can be established which all will recognize—a consummation not now to be hoped for. I believe that this country is alone in referring matters of art to legislative committees. In England committees supervise and report, and Parliament criticizes and condemns, but the artist is not interfered with in his own province. The law maxim is held good in that case. I have been told that the invention of the alto-relievo upon the tympanum was due to Mr. Adams. If so, it was an unhappy exertion of his great powers. Sculpture, when it adorns buildings, is subordinate to them; and when the sculptor invades the tympanum, he must fill it, or he produces a meager and mean effect. Mr. Adams knew all of art that books and much observation could teach him, but he could not, of course, be aware of the many proprieties violated in that invention. The work has another defect as sculpture. It is the translation of rhetoric into stone—a feat often fatal to the rhetoric, always fatal to the stone.

As a most honorable contrast to ever-conflicting claims of private taste and whim to obtain utterance in the public works, I feel pleasure and pride in observing the course adopted by the architect[6] who has been honored with the task of adding the wings of the Cap-

---

[6] [Thomas U. Walter. His predecessor was Benjamin H. Latrobe.]

itol. That architect, trained in the severest school of ancient art, had he been called on for a new building, would surely have attempted something very different from the actual Capitol. Called to enlarge it, he has sought to divest himself of every prepossession that would interfere with its harmony as a whole. He has approached his task with reverence. He has sought to keep company with his predecessor; this is not only honorable and just as regards Latrobe, but can take nothing from his own well-earned reputation. Speaking now and in view of the mere model, I doubt if it be even in his power so widely to extend the façade without painfully isolating the cupola and leaving the present edifice too low, too wanting in mass and weight, to characterize a center. Avoiding this defect, he will triumph over a great obstacle. What the architect has here decided in reference to the original design of the Capitol seems worthy of all emulation on the part of such as, by the vicissitudes of office, may have charge of the national buildings.

In all remarks upon important public edifices there is a twofold subject under contemplation: first, the organic structure of the works; second, their monumental character. To plant a building firmly on the ground; to give it the light that may, the air that must, be needed; to apportion the spaces for convenience, decide their size, and model their shapes for their functions—these acts organize a building. No college of architects is a quorum to judge this part of the task. The occupants alone can say if they have been well served; time alone can stamp any building as solid. The monumental character of a building has reference to its site—to its adaptation in size and form to that site. It has reference also to the external expression of the inward functions of the building—to adaptation of its features and their gradation to its dignity and importance; and it relates, moreover, to that just distinction which taste always requires between external breadth and interior detail.

To ascertain what the organic requirements of a building like the Capitol are, is in itself a most laborious task. To meet them requires all the science we possess. Have we not seen the House of Lords, in spite of all the experience and the knowledge brought to bear upon the vast outlay that reared it, pronounced a gewgaw by the men who were obliged to work therein? Discomfort and annoyance soon find utterance. Decoration and magnificence in such cases, like the velvet and gilding of a ship's cabin, seen with seasick eyes, aggravate our discontent. Nor is a defective arrangement merely uncomfortable; it may prove costly beyond all belief. I have been assured by one of the chief officers of a department that one-half of the employees of his section of the administration were required only by the blundering and ignorant arrangement of the edifice. To say that such oversights are inevitable is an unjust accusation of the art. When those who are called to the task of lodging one of the departments of the Government shall make organization the basis of their design, instead of a predetermined front, which often deserves to have the inverted commas of quotation affixed to it, we shall hear no such complaints as I have above related.

The men who have reduced locomotion to its simplest elements, in the trotting wagon and the yacht *America,* are nearer to Athens at this moment than they who would bend the Greek temple to every use. I contend for Greek principles, not Greek things. If a flat sail goes nearest wind, a bellying sail, though picturesque, must be given up. The slender harness and tall gaunt wheels are not only effective, they are beautiful—for they respect the beauty of a horse, and do not uselessly task him. The English span is a good one, but they lug along more pretension than beauty; they are stopped in their way to claim respect for wealth and station; they are stopped for this, and therefore easily passed by those who care not to seem, but are. To prefer housings to horseflesh, and trappings to men, is alike worthy of a SAVAGE.

THE WASHINGTON MONUMENT

A national monument to Washington has been designed, and is in process of construction. A lithographic print of this design is before the public. It represents an obelisk rising out of a low circular building whose exterior presents a Greek colonnade of the Doric order. A facsimile of the endorsement of some of our most distinguished citizens recommends this design to their fellow countrymen. I propose to examine the invention.

The prominent peculiarity of the design before us is the intermarriage of an Egyptian monument— whether astronomical, as I believe, or phallic, as contended by a Boston critic, matters not very much— with a Greek structure, or one of Greek elements. I do not think it is in the power of art to effect such an amalgamation without corrupting and destroying the special beauties and characters of the two elements. The one, simple even to monotony, may be defined a gigantic expression of unity; the other, a combination of organized parts assembled for a common object. The very perfection of their forms as exponents of so distinct characters makes them protest against juxtaposition.

If the union of Egyptian mass and weight with Greek combination and harmony be heterodox, the order in which they are here displayed is even more strikingly a violation of propriety. The complex, subdivided, comparatively light Greek structure is placed as a basis, a foundation. The Egyptian mass of stone rises above it. When this arrangement is stated, I must think that its palpable absurdity is demonstrated. It may be urged that those weaker and more slender columns veil a massive foundation within them. We had guessed this already, because a miracle alone could otherwise sustain the weight. The *pillars* hide the *strength* of the structure, hence their impertinence as an architectural feature. It is incumbent upon edifices, first, to be strong; secondly, TO LOOK STRONG. We have read of a colossus of brass with feet of clay, and the image is striking. To an architect, Egyptian weight sustained in appearance by Greek pillars is not less so. That buildings, in rising from the earth, be broad and simple at their bases, that they grow lighter not only in fact but in expression as they ascend, is a principle established. The laws of gravitation are at the root of this axiom. The spire obeys it. The obelisk is its simplest expression.

Waiving the impropriety of a Doric colonnade as a basis for an obelisk, I object to that order for a circular structure. The Doric capital, in its upper member, echoes and parallels the entablature. In a circular structure this is impossible without maiming the order. Your capital protests against its entablature. For circular structures—in the temple of Vesta, and that beautiful ruin at Tivoli, for instance,—the Corinthian capital has been adopted; but the Corinthian is too manifestly absurd a basis for a plain shaft of stone.

This obelisk is made to differ essentially from the most admired specimens of that kind of monument. The differences are, first, in the relative diameters at the summit and base; second, in the relative height of the pyramidion which forms the apex. In Cleopatra's Needle the base is a full diagonal of the summit of the prism. In this the base is less than that diagonal. By this departure from example topheaviness has been obtained. The altitude of the pyramidion in Cleopatra's Needle is equal to the width of the base and is, of course, a very acute angle, terminating gradually the lofty shaft. In this the pyramidion forms an obtuse angle, its altitude is so small that a little distance will obliterate it altogether, and the obelisk must assume a truncated and of course unfinished appearance.

When Michelangelo was wending his way from Florence to Rome, to assume the charge of finishing St. Peter's church, his servant related that on reaching the summit of the Apennines near Poggibonsi he turned his horse and sat gazing long and intently upon the dome of Brunelleschi, the giant cupola of the Florentine cathedral. After some time he was heard to growl, "Better than thee, I cannot; like thee, I will not." The result was the dome of St. Peter's. Michelangelo "took the responsibility," as such men always will. He did it at his peril, as all men must. Implicit conformity to precedent obliterates and annihilates the individual; violation of it, not justified by theory, or by practical result, sets the individual on no enviable pedestal. A throne may become a pillory.

The obelisk has to my eye a singular aptitude, in its form and character, to call attention to a spot memorable in history. It says but one word, but it speaks loud. If I understand its voice, it says, Here! It says no more. For this reason it was that I designed an obelisk for Bunker Hill,[7] and urged arguments that appeared to

[7] [To whom credit should be given for the design of the Bunker Hill Monument as it stands, is a question that may never be settled. Greenough, Robert

me unanswerable against a column standing alone.[8] If this be the expression of the obelisk, I object to the site of the proposed monument.

I protest also against the enormous dimensions of this structure. It is another example of the arithmetical sublime—an attempt to realize in art the physical truth that many little things united form one great one; which *in art is not true*. A monolith, a single shaft of granite, has a value like that of the diamond—a value which increases in a geometric ratio with its weight. Why? Because its extraction from the quarry, its elaboration and safe erection, show not only wealth but *science*. The temple of Minerva at Athens, the marvel

Mills, and Solomon Willard have each their champions. Greenough and Mills, either together or separately, favored an obelisk. Willard and Alexander Parris made preliminary designs for a column. Mills later designed the Washington Monument, which is an obelisk, but regretted that the pantheon which he designed for the base—the "crumbling detail" excoriated by Greenough—was not built; both the shafts, he complained, were like "stalks of asparagus." Willard was, at any rate, elected architect of the Bunker Hill Monument, and supervised its erection.]

[8] The column used as a form of monument has two advantages. First, it is a beautiful object—confessedly so. Secondly, it requires no study or thought; the formula being ready made to our hands.

I object, as regards the first of these advantages, that the beauty of a column, perfect as it is, is a relative beauty, and arises from its adaptation to the foundation on which it rests, and to the entablature which it is organized to sustain. The spread of the upper member of the capital calls for the entablature, cries aloud for it. The absence of that burden is expressive either of incompleteness, if the object be fresh and new, or of ruin, if it bear the marks of age. The column is, therefore, essentially fractional—a capital defect in a monument, which should always be independent. I object to the second advantage as being one only to the ignorant and incapable. I hold the chief value of a monument to be this, that it affords opportunity for feeling, of ancient as of modern critics, was scarce larger than one of our schoolhouses. It was great but not large. It was a jewel both of design and structure. It was an embodiment of thought.

To be impressive a monument must contain thought and feeling. *Flendum est primum ipsi tibi!* Your five hundred feet of granite built as chimneys are, stone upon stone, is a failure. It shows how much you are willing to spend to have done with it. "Il faut payer de sa peau!"

A structure which rises five hundred feet from the ground and bears the name of Washington must form a unique feature in this metropolis. It must command

thought, and study, and that it not only occasions these in the architect, but also in the beholder.

I have urged these arguments in conversation, and have sometimes been met by the declaration that my hearer did not *feel* their force as against what he liked in itself. I may state here that such a feeling places him in the same category with those to whom it is indifferent whether a book be held with the right or with the wrong side up. It accuses want of vision or want of instruction.

But ancient Rome possessed two of these monuments, London has two, and Paris has two. To this I will only answer that London and Paris have confessedly followed Rome in this matter, and Rome was more eager to seize upon and appropriate the Greek magnificence than capable of digesting and assimilating it. But the attempting now to argue against columns so universally admired as monuments is presumptuous. I object to this objection that it is not American.

The column used as an integral monument, however its fractional character may be disguised by urns, statues, or other objects placed upon it, belongs to the numerous and respectable family of makeshifts—taking a form or object designed for one purpose, and applying it to another,—which is a violation of the first sublime law of creation. Creation supposes that neither material nor power is wanting.

the attention of everyone, be he American or foreigner, who sees its lofty shaft towering into the blue and holding the sunshine after twilight is gray below. What will be its effect artistically speaking? Kneading into incongruous contact elements hitherto only jumbled by conquest and ruin—truncated—bare—without gradation and without finale—standing upon crumbling detail—heavy above and light below—it will be a symbol of huge aspiration and chaotic impotence.

Monuments to really great men are opportunities on which to hang the proofs of the development of art. The great need them not. We need them. The tombs of the Medici embody the theory of Buonarroti. The statue of Frederick[9] is the apotheosis of Prussian sculpture.

The obelisk which stands at the entrance of the Champs Élysées is typical of African conquest. Like the captive elephants led in a Roman show, its exotic form gives significance to the triumph that placed it there. The monoliths that tower before the Roman basilicas have also a certain propriety in the residence of an absolute temporal prince who is at the same time assumed to be the vicar of Christ. All forms may be collected without, as all tongues are spoken within.

[9] [Rauch's "Frederick the Great," in Berlin.]

I am aware that there is scarce an architect in the country that could not have demonstrated the absurdity of the monument I have examined, and have thus prevented its consummation. Why were they all silent?

THE EMBARKATION OF THE PILGRIMS
[WEIR'S HISTORICAL PAINTING]

The general aspect of this picture is striking. The idea of representing these heroes of our history engaged in prayer on the deck of the good ship that was to waft them to these shores was an ingenious and a happy one. The composition of lines is worthy of Mr. Weir[10] and shows a profound study of that very difficult branch of his art. There is no claptrap or vulgar effect in the arrangement—all are in their places, and a pleasing variety has been created without any theatrical makeshift. The subject has been treated with due reverence—conscientiously. It is a work of good omen.

The arrangement of the chiaroscuro is a puzzle to my understanding. I see a circle of light enclosing a broad mass of half shadow. In this half shadow lies the

---

[10] [Robert W. Weir's paintings included several on American historical themes. This one hangs in the rotunda of the National Capitol. It is illustrated on page 120, with key to its figures on page 121, of Chas. E. Fairman's *Art and Artists of the Capitol* .]

pith and marrow of the subject matter of this composition. He who prays—he who holds the sacred volume—the mother with her ailing child—all these are in twilight, while the evidence and flash of day are reserved for figures half averted—piebald silks, and gleaming armor, with other objects essentially accessory.

If any deep-laid train be here to rouse the attention and chain it to the important features of this page, it has missed its object with me. I long to haul a sail aside, if sail it be that makes this mischief, and let in a shaft of light upon that prayerful face. I am out of humor with that dress, so real, which mocks my desire to see men. The armor is true Milan steel. The men are foggy. The sail is real—the maker would swear to his stitches. The hobnailed shoes are so new and actual that I smell leather as I stand there. To balance the execution, the hair should be less conventional—the flesh, too, more transparent and lifelike. I see no gleam from any eye in all that company; but the iron ring in yonder foot of the sail twinkles ambitiously. This inversion of the true law of emphasis is unaccountable to me in this master. Had I any hope of influencing him, I would beg of him, while yet it is day, to modify the effect of this work. If I despaired of bringing the heads and hands up to the still life, I would put the latter down, not only in light but in elaboration and illusion, until it kept its place.

Light in a composition is like sound and emphasis in delivery. You may make a figure or a group tell darkly amid a glare for certain purposes; not when the nuances of physiognomy and emotion are essential. Awfully have I seen in a broad illuminated group a cloud darken Judas as he gave the traitor kiss to our Lord. The masters of Venice have more than once succeeded in giving to figures in shadow all the roundness, glow, and reality admitted in the highest light; where that power of pencil is, who could deny the right *quidlibet audendi*? To my sense, here are figures more important than these on the foreground, which are flat, and cold, and dim.

Who can doubt that Mr. Weir, had he lived in an age and country where art was prized, would have wrought many great, instead of this one very respectable picture? I mean for the government.

As I have ventured to complain of the Flemish illusion and microscopic finish of the accessories in this picture, contrasted as they are by an execution rather dim and vague in the chief figures, I will further explain my meaning by a contrary example in a masterpiece of ancient art. In the group of Laocoön we never weary of admiring the palpitating agony of the father, the helpless struggles of the sons. The serpents, which are the causes of this pain and despair, are scarce noticed; why? because the artist wished to chain our attention upon the *human* portion of the spectacle. He had no means of veiling the snakes in shadow; but he has veiled them in the mode of treatment. There is more imitation, undercutting, illusion, in one of the gray locks of the old man than in the serpents' whole form. Even their heads as they strike are made vague and indistinct. Do we suppose that the sculptor who made those limbs throb, and that marble mouth hot with pain, was blind to the beauty of the bossed hide and abdominal rings of a snake? This is impossible. He gave only enough of the snakes to tell the story, because the snakes were not subjects of his chisel, but the men. This is art; nay, this is pure art.

The same rule, or a rule analogous to this, decides the treatment of drapery in the higher works of Greece. In decorative statuary the Greek showed his feeling for all the minutest graces and the most accidental effects of varied stuffs; and his hand echoed his eye, and mirrored the whole in stone. But in his great works the stuff is one, and all the folds are wrought broad and simple. He avoids *small facts* that he may fasten your eye upon *great truth*. To be true to fact the figure of Laocoön should be clothed in a priest's dress—clothe him thus and the subject is for a painter. The first postulate of sculpture in its essence is that the veil of convention be rent. Dress the fighting gladiator and you might as well sculpture a house and tell me that a fighting hero is inside thereof; or say, as Michelangelo playfully said, that perfection lies in every rock that rolls from a quarry. True it is that perfect beauty is in every rock; the art lies in stripping therefrom the dress of chips that disguise it.

There is one law of painting, as of sculpture, which he alone can fully understand and obey who is conversant with both arts. This law commands, to lay the stress of study there where the art is strong, and avoid, as far as may be, the occasion of showing its impotence. For instance, when in the fifteenth century they attempted perspective in bas-relief, they blundered; because the success is partial, and unable to keep company with painted perspective, where it is perfect. The flying hair and waving draperies of Bernini are similar proofs of ill-judged toil. They are a conquest of mechanical difficulty, and so is the Chinese ivory ball within ball—both belong to the same family, characterized by Reynolds as laborious effects of idleness; both are curious and amusing, and so is a juggler—but not in the Senate.

THE SMITHSONIAN INSTITUTION

I was wandering, the evening of my arrival in Washington, after a nine years' absence; musing as I walked, I found myself on the banks of the Potomac. I was reflecting upon the singular contrast between the non-committal, negative nomenclature of these avenues and streets and the sagacious policy which in Europe makes every name a monument, every square enforce the creed, every bridge echo a historical fact, or record a triumph of principle. Nature in the moral world still abhors a vacuum, and I felt that A, B, C street were temporary names—squatters, waiting till the rightful lords of the domain shall appear.

I pondered in my mind the structure of a monument which should record the labors, sufferings, and triumph of the champions of freedom;—of free thought and belief, of free speech and free action. The moon was rising, half veiled by long straight bars of heavy cloud. She rose out of them and her light fell broad and bright on the distant Capitol, with triple dome and stately columns. My eagerness to rear the pile I had been dreaming of was hushed. I thought I saw it there before me! Those pillars were no more mere shafts of stone; Luther and Melancthon, Russell, Hampden, Galileo, Savonarola, Sarpi, and a host besides, united in spectral majesty with the worthies of our own land to uphold the roof! The whole was cemented with the blood of martyrs. No man that had cast fear behind him, and done battle for the right, but had given his grain to form that temple. It stirred me, for I am not used to the sight. A few weeks earlier I had been seated beside a pale Dominican friar in the cell where Savonarola dwelt, and where hung a picture of the Puritan of the Arno burning on the great square and steadied amid the flames by masked monks as he reeled amid the choking heat; I thought how different is the fire that here burns. As a mere unit of humanity I felt consoled. Suddenly, as I walked, the dark form of the Smithsonian palace rose between me and the white Capitol, and I stopped. Tower and battlement, and all that medieval confusion, stamped itself on the halls of Congress, as ink on paper! Dark on that whiteness— complication on that simplicity! It scared me. Was it a specter, or was not I another Rip Van Winkle who had slept too long? It seemed to threaten. It seemed to say, I bide my time! Oh, it was indeed monastic at that hour!

I never was of those who hold that there is a covered way from the Vatican to Avernus, on the one hand, corresponding to that which leads to the Castel Sant' Angelo, on the other. I have seen the Italian clergy nearly—sometimes intimately,—from the prelate to the begging friar; I have admired their scholars, and have loved their men. I revere the bridge over which our faith has been borne to us. I am not so ignorant of history as to repudiate the sagacious preservers of the old Latin civilization. Still, I have brought from that land a fear of their doctrine and a hatred of their politics. I fear their doctrine because it seems to lull and to benumb the general, the average mind, while it rouses and spurs the few. I fear it the more because others do not fear it. I hate their politics because they are hostile to ours.

This it as that made me shudder at that dark pile— that castle of authority—that outwork of prescription. On walking round to the south, I was much relieved; I could see through and through the building. This was a departure from all that I had seen in the real, old, turreted fortresses of theology. It was of good omen.

I am not about to criticize the edifice. I have not quite recovered from my alarm. There is still a certain mystery about those towers and steep belfries that makes me uneasy. This is a practical land. They must be for something. Is no *coup d'état* lurking there? Can they be merely ornaments, like the tassels to a university cap? Perhaps they are an allopathic dose administered to that parsimony which so long denied to science where to lay her head—*contraria contrariis curantur!* They must have cost much money.

"Bosom'd high in tufted trees," the Smithsonian College must, in itself, be hereafter a most picturesque object—the models whence it has been imitated are both "rich and rare"—the connoisseurs may well "wonder how the devil it got *there*."

I propose to examine the building hereafter, with reference to its organization for a distinct purpose.

Remarks on American Art

THE SUSCEPTIBILITY, THE tastes, and the genius which enable a people to enjoy the fine arts and to excel in them have been denied to the Anglo-Americans, not only by European talkers, but by European thinkers. The assertion of our obtuseness and inefficiency in this respect has been ignorantly and presumptuously set forth by some persons merely to fill up the measure of our condemnation. Others have arrived at the same conclusion after examining our political and social character, after investigating our exploits, and testing our capacities. They admit that we trade with enterprise and skill, that we build ships cunningly and sail them well, that we have a quick and farsighted apprehension of the value of a territory, that we make wholesome homespun laws for its government, and that we fight hard when molested in any of these homely exercises of our ability; but they assert that there is a stubborn, antipoetical tendency in all that we do or say or think; they attribute our very excellence in the ordinary business of life to causes which must prevent our development as artists.

Enjoying the accumulated result of the thought and labor of centuries, Europe has witnessed our struggles with the hardships of an untamed continent and the disadvantages of colonial relations with but a partial appreciation of what we aim at, with but an imperfect knowledge of what we have done. Seeing us intently occupied during several generations in felling forests, building towns, and constructing roads, she thence formed a theory that we are good for nothing except these pioneer efforts. She taunted us because there were no statues or frescoes in our log cabins; she pronounced us unmusical because we did not sit down in the swamp, with an Indian on one side and a rattlesnake on the other, to play the violin. That she should triumph over the deficiencies of a people who had set the example of revolt and republicanism was natural; but the reason which she assigned for those deficiencies was not the true reason. She argued with the depth and the sagacity of a philosopher who should conclude from seeing an infant imbibe with eagerness its first aliment that its whole life would be occupied in similar absorption.

Sir Walter Scott, rank tory as he was, showed more good sense when, in recommending an American book to Miss Edgeworth, he accounted for such a phenomenon by saying that "people once possessed of a three-legged stool soon contrive to make an easy chair." Humble as the phrase is, we here perceive an expectation on his part that the energies now exercised in laying the foundations of a mighty empire would, in due time, rear the stately columns of civilization and crown the edifice with the entablature of letters and of arts. Remembering that one leg of the American stool was planted in Maine, a second in Florida, and the third at the base of the Rocky Mountains, he could scarce expect that the chair would become an easy one in a half-century.

It is true that, before the Declaration of Independence, Copley had in Boston formed a style of portrait which filled Sir Joshua Reynolds with astonishment; and that West, breaking through the bar of Quaker prohibition and conquering the prejudice against a provincial aspirant, had taken a high rank in the highest walk of art in London. Stuart, Trumbull, Allston, Morse, Leslie, and Newton followed in quick succession, while Vanderlyn won golden opinions at Rome and bore away high honors at Paris. So far were the citizens of the Republic from showing a want of capacity for art that we may safely affirm the bent of their genius was rather peculiarly in that direction, since the first burins of Europe were employed in the service of the American pencil before Irving had written and while Cooper was yet a child. That England, with these facts before her, should have accused us of obtuseness in regard to art, and that we should have pleaded guilty to the charge, furnishes the strongest proof of her disposition to underrate our intellectual powers, and of our own ultra-docility and want of self-reliance.

Not many years since, one of the illustrious and good men of America exclaimed, in addressing the nation:

"Excudent alii spirantia mollius aera,
Credo equidem, vivos ducent de marmore voltus!"[1]

Since that period, art has received a new impulse among us. Artists have arisen in numbers; the public gives its attention to their productions; their labors are liberally rewarded. It seems now admitted that wealth

[1] [*Aeneid*, VI, 847–848.]

and cultivation are destined to yield in America the same fruits that they have given in Italy, in Spain, in France, Germany, and England. It seems now admitted that there is no anomalous defect in our mental endowments; that the same powers displayed in clearing the forest and tilling the farm will trim the garden. It seems clear that we are destined to have a school of art.

It becomes a matter of importance to decide how the youth who devote themselves to these studies are to acquire the rudiments of imitation, and what influences are to be made to act upon them. This question seemed, at one time, to have been decided. The friends of art in America looked to Europe for an example; and with the natural assumption that experience had made the Old World wise, in what relates to the fine arts, determined upon forming academies, as the more refined nations of the Continent have ended by doing. We might as well have proposed a national church establishment. That the youth must be taught is clear—but, in framing an institution for that object, if we look to countries grown old in European systems, it must be for warning rather than for example. We speak from long experience and much observation of European academies. We entertain the highest respect for the professional ability and for the personal characters of the gentlemen who preside over those institutions. Nay, it is our conviction of their capacity and of their individual willingness to impart knowledge which forces upon us the opinion of the rottenness of the systems of which they are the instruments.

De Tocqueville remarks upon the British aristocracy that, notwithstanding their sagacity as a body and their integrity and high-toned character as individuals, they have gradually absorbed everything and left the people nothing; while he declares the American employees, though they are sometimes defaulters and dishonest, yet, after all, get little beyond their dues, and are obliged to sacrifice both reputation and self-respect in order to obtain that little. Those who direct the academies of fine arts in Europe are prone to take an advantage of their position analogous to that enjoyed by the aforesaid aristocracy. As the latter come to regard the mass as a flock to be fed, and defended, and cherished, for the sake of their wool and mutton, so the former are not slow to make a band of educandi the basis of a hierarchy. Systems and manner soon usurp the place of sound precept. Faith is insisted on rather than works. The pupils are required to be not only docile, but submissive. They are not free.

To minds once opened to the light of knowledge, an adept may speak in masses, and the seed will fall on good ground; but to awaken a dormant soul, to impart first principles, to watch the budding of the germ of rare talent, requires a contact and relations such as no professor can have with a class, such as few men can have with any boy. If Europe must furnish a model of artistical tuition, let us go at once to the records of the great age of art in Italy, and we shall there learn that Michelangelo and Raphael, and their teachers also, were formed without any of the cumbrous machinery and mill-horse discipline of a modern academy. They were instructed, it is true; they were apprenticed to painters. Instead of passively listening to an experienced proficient merely, they discussed with their fellow students the merits of different works, the advantages of rival methods, the choice between contradictory authorities. They formed one another. Sympathy warmed them, opposition strengthened, and emulation spurred them on. In these latter days, classes of boys toil through the rudiments under the eye of men who are themselves aspirants for the public favor, and who, deriving no benefit, as masters of their apprentices, from the proficiency of the lads, look upon every clever graduate as a stumbling-block in their

45

own way. Hence their system of stupefying discipline, their tying down the pupil to mere manual execution, their silence in regard to principles, their cold reception of all attempts to invent. To chill in others the effort to acquire is in them the instinctive action of a wish to retain. Well do we remember the expression of face and the tone of voice with which one of these bashaws of a European academy once received our praise of the labors of a man grown gray in the practice of his art, but who, though his works were known and admired at Naples and St. Petersburg, at London and Vienna, had not yet won from the powers that were his *exequatur*— "Yes, sir, yes! clever boy, sir! *promises well!*"

The president and the professors of an academy are regarded by the public as, of course, at the head of their respective professions. Their works are models, their opinions give the law. The youth are awed and dazzled by their titles and their fame; the man of genius finds them arrayed in solid phalanx to combat his claim. In those countries where a court bestows all encouragement it is found easy to keep from those in power all knowledge of a dangerous upstart talent. How far this mischievous influence can be carried may be gathered from the position in which Sir Joshua Reynolds and *his court* managed to keep men like Wilson and Gainsborough. He who sees the productions of these men in company with those of their contemporaries, and who remembers the impression which Sir Joshua's writings had conveyed of their standing as artists, will perceive with surprise that they were not the victims of any overt act of misrepresentation, but that they were quietly and gently praised out of the rank due to them into an inferior one, by a union of real talent, constituted influence, and a sly, cool, consistent management.

Many of the ablest painters and sculptors of Europe have expressed to us, directly and frankly, the opinion that academies, furnished though they be with all the means to form the eye, the hand, and the mind of the pupil, are positively hindrances instead of helps to art.

The great element of execution, whether in painting or in sculpture, is imitation. This is the language of art. Almost all clever boys can learn this to a degree far beyond what is supposed. That objects should be placed before them calculated to attract their attention and teach them the rules of proportion while they educate the eye to form and color, no one will dispute; but the insisting upon a routine, the depriving them of all choice or volition, the giving a false preference to readiness of hand over power of thought, all these are great evils, and we fully believe that they fall with a withering force on those minds especially whose nourishment and guidance they were intended to secure—we mean on those minds which are filled with a strong yearning after excellence, warm sympathies, quick, delicate, and nice perceptions, strong will, and a proud consciousness of creative power of mind, joined to diffidence of their capacity to bring into action the energies they feel within them. The paltry prizes offered for the best performances seldom rouse men of this order; they may create in such souls an unamiable contempt for their unsuccessful competitors; they may give to successful mediocrity inflated hopes and a false estimate of its own powers. As a substantial help they are worthless even to the tyro who wins them.

Leonardo da Vinci coiled a rope in his studio and drew from it with the subtlest outline the most elaborate study of light and shade. "Behold!" said he, "my academy!" He meant to show that the elements of art can be learned without the pompous array of the antique school or the lectures of the professor. Few will be tempted to follow his example; but even that were far better than a routine of instruction which, after years of drudgery and labor, sends forth the genius and the blockhead so nearly on a level with each other, the one manacled with precepts, the other armed with them at all points.

The foregoing reflections have been drawn from us by the oft-repeated expression of regret which we have listened to, that "from the constitution of our society, and the nature of our institutions, no influences can be brought to bear upon art with the vivifying power of court patronage." We fully and firmly believe that these institutions are more favorable to a natural, healthful growth of art than any hotbed culture whatever. We cannot (as did Napoleon) make, by a few imperial edicts, an army of battle painters, a hierarchy of drum-and-fife glorifiers. Nor can we, in the lifetime of an individual, so stimulate this branch of culture, so unduly and disproportionately endow it, as to make a Valhalla start from a republican soil. The monuments, the pictures, the statues of the Republic will represent what the people love and wish for—not what they can be made to accept, not how much taxation they will bear. We hope, by such slow growth, to avoid the reaction resulting from a morbid development; a reaction like that which attended the building of St. Peter's; a reaction like that consequent upon the outlay which gave birth to the royal mushroom at Versailles; a reaction like that which we anticipate in Bavaria, unless the people of that country are constituted differently from the rest of mankind.

If there be any youth toiling through the rudiments of art at the forms of the simple and efficient school at New York (whose title is the only pompous thing about it) with a chilling belief that elsewhere the difficulties he struggles with are removed or modified, we call upon him to be of good cheer and to believe—what from our hearts we are convinced of—that there is at present no country where the development and growth of an artist is more free, healthful, and happy than it is in these United States. It is not until the tyro becomes a proficient—nay, an adept—that his fortitude and his temper are put to tests more severe than elsewhere— tests of which we propose to speak more at large on a future occasion.

American Architecture*

W E HAVE HEARD THE LEARNED
in matters relating to art express the opinion that these
United States are destined to form a new style of architecture. Remembering that a vast population, rich in
material and guided by the experience, the precepts,
and the models of the Old World, was about to erect
durable structures for every function of civilized life,
we also cherished the hope that such a combination
would speedily be formed.

---

* [In *English Traits* (1856), Emerson said of this essay that it "announced
in advance the leading thoughts of Mr. Ruskin on the *morality* in architecture, notwithstanding the antagonism of their views of the history of art."
Greenough's "American Architecture" was first published in 1843, in the
United States Magazine and Democratic Review. Ruskin's *Seven Lamps of
Architecture,* in which he indicated his idea that the buildings and art of a
people express their morality, first appeared in 1849.]

We forgot that, though the country was young, yet the people were old; that as Americans we have no childhood, no half-fabulous, legendary wealth, no misty, cloud-enveloped background. We forgot that we had not unity of religious belief, nor unity of origin; that our territory, extending from the white bear to the alligator, made our occupations dissimilar, our character and tastes various. We forgot that the Republic had leaped full-grown and armed to the teeth from the brain of her parent, and that a hammer had been the instrument of delivery. We forgot that reason had been the dry nurse of the giant offspring, and had fed her from the beginning with the strong bread and meat of fact; that every wry face the bantling ever made had been daguerreotyped, and all her words and deeds printed and labeled away in the pigeonholes of official bureaus.

Reason can dissect, but cannot originate; she can adopt, but cannot create; she can modify, but cannot find. Give her but a cockboat, and she will elaborate a line-of-battle ship; give her but a beam with its wooden tooth, and she turns out the patent plow. She is not young; and when her friends insist upon the phenomena of youth, then is she least attractive. She can imitate the flush of the young cheek, but where is the flash of the young eye? She buys the teeth—alas! she cannot buy the breath of childhood. The puny cathedral of Broadway,[1] like an elephant dwindled to the size of a dog, measures her yearning for Gothic sublimity, while the roar of the Astor House, and the mammoth vase of the great reservoir, shows how she works when she feels at home and is in earnest.

The mind of this country has never been seriously applied to the subject of building. Intently engaged in matters of more pressing importance, we have been content to receive our notions of architecture as we have received the fashion of our garments and the form of our entertainments, from Europe. In our eagerness to appropriate, we have neglected to adapt, to distinguish,—nay, to understand. We have built small Gothic temples of wood and have omitted all ornaments for economy, unmindful that size, material, and ornament are the elements of effect in that style of building. Captivated by the classic symmetry of the Athenian models, we have sought to bring the Parthenon into our streets, to make the temple of Theseus work in our towns.[2] We have shorn them of their lateral colonnades, let them down from their dignified platform, pierced

---

[1] [The reference is apparently to Trinity Church, which was completed in 1846. Trinity is a sizable church, but puny if compared with the great European cathedrals.]

[2] ["The public sentiment just now runs almost exclusively and popularly into the Grecian school. We build little besides temples for our churches, our

their walls for light, and, instead of the storied relief and the eloquent statue which enriched the frieze and graced the pediment, we have made our chimneytops to peer over the broken profile and tell, by their rising smoke, of the traffic and desecration of the interior. Still the model may be recognized, some of the architectural features are entire; like the captive king, stripped alike of arms and purple and drudging amid the Helots of a capital, the Greek temple, as seen among us, claims pity for its degraded majesty, and attests the barbarian force which has abused its nature and been blind to its qualities.

If we trace architecture from its perfection in the days of Pericles to its manifest decay in the reign of Constantine, we shall find that one of the surest symptoms of decline was the adoption of admired forms and models for purposes not contemplated in their invention. The forum became a temple; the tribunal became a temple; the theater was turned into a church; nay, the column, that organized member, that subordinate part, set up for itself, usurped unity, and was a monument! The great principles of architecture being once abandoned, correctness gave way to novelty, economy

banks, our taverns, our court-houses, and our dwellings. A friend of mine has just built a brewery on the model of the Temple of the Winds."—Aristabulus Bragg, in Cooper's novel, *Home As Found* (1838).]

and vainglory associated produced meanness and pretension. Sculpture, too, had waned. The degenerate workmen could no longer match the fragments they sought to mingle, nor copy the originals they only hoped to repeat. The moldering remains of better days frowned contempt upon such impotent efforts, till, in the gradual coming of darkness, ignorance became contempt, and insensibility ceased to compare.

We say that the mind of this country has never been seriously applied to architecture. True it is that the commonwealth, with that desire of public magnificence which has ever been a leading feature of democracy, has called from the vasty deep of the past the spirits of the Greek, the Roman, and the Gothic styles; but they would not come when she did call to them! The vast cathedral, with its ever-open portals, towering high above the courts of kings, inviting all men to its cool and fragrant twilight, where the voice of the organ stirs the blood, and the dim-seen visions of saints and martyrs bleed and die upon the canvas amid the echoes of hymning voices and the clouds of frankincense—this architectural embodying of the divine and blessed words, "Come to me, ye who labor and are heavy laden, and I will give you rest!" demands a sacrifice of what we hold dearest. Its cornerstone must be laid upon the right to judge the claims of the church. The style of Greek architecture, as seen in the Greek temple, demands the aid of sculpture, insists upon every feature of its original organization, loses its harmony if a note be dropped in the execution, and when so modified as to serve for a customhouse or bank, departs from its original beauty and propriety as widely as the crippled gelding of a hackney coach differs from the bounding and neighing wild horse of the desert. Even where, in the fervor of our faith in shapes, we have sternly adhered to the dictum of another age, and have actually succeeded in securing the entire exterior which echoes the forms of Athens, the pile stands a stranger among us, and receives a respect akin to what we should feel for a fellow citizen in the garb of Greece. It is a make-believe. It is not the real thing. We see the marble capitals; we trace the acanthus leaves of a celebrated model—incredulous;[a] it is not a temple.

The number and variety of our experiments in building show the dissatisfaction of the public taste with what has been hitherto achieved; the expense at which they have been made proves how strong is the yearning after excellence; the talents and acquire-

[a] [In Greenough's pseudonymous *Travels* this is "incredulous odi," for *incredulus odi* in Horace's line, "Quodcunque ostendis mihi sic incredulus odi" ("Scenes put before me in this way move only my incredulity and disgust").]

56

ments of the artists whose services have been engaged in them are such as to convince us that the fault lies in the system, not in the men. Is it possible that out of this chaos order can arise?—that of these conflicting dialects and jargons a language can be born? When shall we have done with experiments? What refuge is there from the absurdities that have successively usurped the name and functions of architecture? Is it not better to go on with consistency and uniformity, in imitation of an admired model, than incur the disgrace of other failures? In answering these questions let us remember with humility that all salutary changes are the work of many and of time; but let us encourage experiment at the risk of license, rather than submit to an iron rule that begins by sacrificing reason, dignity, and comfort. Let us consult nature, and in the assurance that she will disclose a mine richer than was ever dreamed of by the Greeks, in art as well as in philosophy. Let us regard as ingratitude to the author of nature the despondent idleness that sits down while one want is unprovided for, one worthy object unattained.

If, as the first step in our search after the great principles of construction, we but observe the skeletons and skins of animals, through all the varieties of beast and bird, of fish and insect, are we not as forcibly struck by their variety as by their beauty? There is no arbitrary law of proportion, no unbending model of form. There is scarce a part of the animal organization which we do not find elongated or shortened, increased, diminished, or suppressed, as the wants of the genus or species dictate, as their exposure or their work may require. The neck of the swan and that of the eagle, however different in character and proportion, equally charm the eye and satisfy the reason. We approve the length of the same member in grazing animals, its shortness in beasts of prey. The horse's shanks are thin, and we admire them; the greyhound's chest is deep, and we cry, beautiful! It is neither the presence nor the absence of this or that part, or shape, or color, that wins our eye in natural objects; it is the consistency and harmony of the parts juxtaposed, the subordination of details to masses, and of masses to the whole.

The law of adaptation is the fundamental law of nature in all structure. So unflinchingly does she modify a type in accordance with a new position, that some philosophers have declared a variety of appearance to be the object aimed at; so entirely does she limit the modification to the demands of necessity, that adherence to one original plan seems, to limited intelligence, to be carried to the very verge of caprice. The domination of arbitrary rules of taste has produced the very counterpart of the wisdom thus displayed in every object around us; we tie up the camelopard to the rack; we shave the lion, and call him a dog; we strive to bind the unicorn with his band in the furrow, and make him harrow the valleys after us!

When the savage of the South Sea islands shapes his war club, his first thought is of its use. His first efforts pare the long shaft, and mold the convenient handle; then the heavier end takes gradually the edge that cuts, while it retains the weight that stuns. His idler hour divides its surface by lines and curves, or embosses it with figures that have pleased his eye or are linked with his superstition. We admire its effective shape, its Etruscan-like quaintness, its graceful form and subtle outline, yet we neglect the lesson it might teach. If we compare the form of a newly invented machine with the perfected type of the same instrument, we observe, as we trace it through the phases of improvement, how weight is shaken off where strength is less needed, how functions are made to approach without impeding each other, how straight becomes curved, and the curve is straightened, till the straggling and cumbersome machine becomes the compact, effective, and beautiful engine.

So instinctive is the perception of organic beauty in the human eye, that we cannot withhold our admiration even from the organs of destruction. There is majesty in the royal paw of the lion, music in the motion of the brindled tiger; we accord our praise to the sword and the dagger, and shudder our approval of the frightful aptitude of the ghastly guillotine.

Conceiving destruction to be a normal element of the system of nature equally with production, we have used the word beauty in connection with it. We have no objection to exchange it for the word character, as indicating the mere adaptation of forms to functions, and would gladly substitute the actual pretensions of our architecture to the former, could we hope to secure the latter.

Let us now turn to a structure of our own, one which, from its nature and uses, commands us to reject authority, and we shall find the result of the manly use of plain good sense, so like that of taste, and genius too, as scarce to require a distinctive title. Observe a ship at sea! Mark the majestic form of her hull as she rushes through the water, observe the graceful bend of her body, the gentle transition from round to flat, the grasp of her keel, the leap of her bows, the symmetry and rich tracery of her spars and rigging, and those grand wind muscles, her sails. Behold an organization second only to that of an animal, obedient as the horse, swift as the stag, and bearing the burden of a thousand camels from pole to pole! What academy of design, what research of connoisseurship, what imitation of the Greeks produced this marvel of construction? Here is the result of the study of man upon the great deep, where Nature spake of the laws of building, not in the feather and in the flower, but in winds and waves, and he bent all his mind to hear and to obey.[4] Could we carry into our civil architecture the responsibilities that weigh upon our shipbuilding, we should ere long have edifices as superior to the Parthenon, for the purposes that we require, as the *Constitution* or the *Pennsylvania* is to the galley of the Argonauts. Could our blunders on terra firma be put to the same dread test that those of shipbuilders are, little would be now left to say on this subject.

Instead of forcing the functions of every sort of building into one general form, adopting an outward shape for the sake of the eye or of association, without

[4] [Greenough would not allow a figurehead, certainly not a carved wooden statue painted in imitation of marble, as an embellishment to a ship. Having remarked one that had lost both arms and a leg, he wrote: "I was delighted with another proof that I had found of the perfect organization of ships, viz., that the only part of the hull where function will allow a statue to stand without being in Jack's way is one where the plunge bath so soon demolishes it."— *Travels*, p. 179.]

reference to the inner distribution, let us begin from the heart as the nucleus, and work outward. The most convenient size and arrangement of the rooms that are to constitute the building being fixed, the access of the light that may, of the air that must be wanted, being provided for, we have the skeleton of our building. Nay, we have all excepting the dress. The connection and order of parts, juxtaposed for convenience, cannot fail to speak of their relation and uses. As a group of idlers on the quay, if they grasp a rope to haul a vessel to the pier, are united in harmonious action by the cord they seize, as the slowly yielding mass forms a thorough-bass to their livelier movement, so the unflinching adaptation of a building to its position and use gives, as a sure product of that adaptation, character and expression.

What a field of study would be opened by the adoption in civil architecture of those laws of apportionment, distribution, and connection which we have thus hinted at? No longer could the mere tyro huddle together a crowd of ill-arranged, ill-lighted, and stifled rooms and, masking the chaos with the sneaking copy of a Greek façade, usurp the name of architect. If this anatomic connection and proportion has been attained in ships, in machines, and, in spite of false principles, in such buildings as made a departure from it fatal, as in bridges and in scaffolding, why should we fear its immediate use in all construction? As its first result, the bank would have the physiognomy of a bank, the church would be recognized as such, nor would the billiard room and the chapel wear the same uniform of columns and pediment. The African king, standing in mock majesty with his legs and feet bare, and his body clothed in a cast coat of the Prince Regent, is an object whose ridiculous effect defies all power of face. Is not the Greek temple jammed in between the brick shops of Wall Street or Cornhill, covered with lettered signs, and occupied by groups of money-changers and applewomen, a parallel even for his African majesty?

We have before us a letter in which Mr. Jefferson recommends the model of the Maison Carrée for the State House at Richmond. Was he aware that the Maison Carrée is but a fragment, and that, too, of a Roman temple? He was; it is beautiful—is the answer. An English society erected in Hyde Park a cast in bronze of the colossal Achilles of the Quirinal, and, changing the head, transformed it into a monument to Wellington. But where is the distinction between the personal prowess, the invulnerable body, the heaven-shielded safety of the hero of the Iliad and the complex of qualities which makes the modern general? The statue is beautiful—is the answer. If such reasoning is to hold, why not translate one of Pindar's odes in memory of Washington, or set up in Carolina a colossal Osiris in honor of General Greene?

The monuments of Egypt and of Greece are sublime as expressions of their power and their feeling. The modern nation that appropriates them displays only wealth in so doing. The possession of means, not accompanied by the sense of propriety or feeling for the true, can do no more for a nation than it can do for an individual. The want of an illustrious ancestry may be compensated, fully compensated; but the purloining of the coat-of-arms of a defunct family is intolerable. That such a monument as we have described should have been erected in London while Chantrey flourished, when Flaxman's fame was cherished by the few, and Baily and Behnes were already known, is an instructive fact. That the illustrator of the Greek poets and of the Lord's Prayer should in the meanwhile have been preparing designs for George the Fourth's silversmiths, is not less so.

The edifices in whose construction the principles of architecture are developed may be classed as organic, formed to meet the wants of their occupants, or monumental, addressed to the sympathies, the faith, or the taste of a people. These two great classes of buildings, embracing almost every variety of structure, though occasionally joined and mixed in the same edifice, have their separate rules, as they have a distinct abstract nature. In the former class the laws of structure and apportionment, depending on definite wants, obey a demonstrable rule. They may be called machines each individual of which must be formed with reference to the abstract type of its species. The individuals of the latter class, bound by no other laws than those of the sentiment which inspires them, and the sympathies to which they are addressed, occupy the positions and assume the forms best calculated to render their parent feeling. No limits can be put to their variety; their size and richness have always been proportioned to the means of the people who have erected them.

If, from what has been thus far said, it shall have appeared that we regard the Greek masters as aught less than the true apostles of correct taste in building, we have been misunderstood. We believe firmly and fully that they can teach us; but let us learn principles, not copy shapes; let us imitate them like men, and not ape them like monkeys. Remembering what a school of art it was that perfected their system of ornament, let us rather adhere to that system in enriching what we invent than substitute novelty for propriety. After observing the innovations of the ancient Romans, and of the modern Italian masters in this department, we cannot but recur to the Horatian precept—

"exemplaria Graeca
Nocturna versate manu, versate diurna!"

To conclude: The fundamental laws of building found at the basis of every style of architecture must be the basis of ours. The adaptation of the forms and magnitude of structures to the climate they are exposed to, and the offices for which they are intended, teaches us to study our own varied wants in these respects.[5] The harmony of their ornaments with the nature that they embellished, and the institutions from which they sprang, calls on us to do the like justice to our country, our government, and our faith. As a Christian preacher may give weight to truth, and add per-

---

[5] ["The fault just now is perhaps to consult the books too rigidly, and to trust too little to invention; for no architecture, and especially no domestic architecture, can ever be above reproach, until climate, the uses of the edifice, and the situation, are respected as leading considerations. Nothing can be uglier, *per se*, than a Swiss cottage, or anything more beautiful under its precise circumstances. As regards these mushroom temples which are the offspring of Mammon, let them be dedicated to whom they may, I should exactly reverse the opinion and say, that while nothing can be much more beautiful, *per se*, nothing can be in worse taste than to put them where they are."—Cooper's *Home As Found* (1838).]

suasion to proof, by studying the models of pagan writers, so the American builder by a truly philosophic investigation of ancient art will learn of the Greeks to be American.

The system of building we have hinted at cannot be formed in a day. It requires all the science of any country to ascertain and fix the proportions and arrangements of the members of a great building, to plant it safely on the soil, to defend it from the elements, to add the grace and poetry of ornament to its frame. Each of these requisites to a good building requires a special study and a lifetime. Whether we are destined soon to see so noble a fruit may be doubtful; but we can, at least, break the ground and throw in the seed.

We are fully aware that many regard all matters of taste as matters of pure caprice and fashion. We are aware that many think our architecture already perfect; but we have chosen, during this sultry weather, to exercise a truly American right—the right of talking. This privilege, thank God, is unquestioned—from Miller,[6] who, robbing Béranger, translates into fanatical prose, "Finissons-en! le monde est assez vieux!" to Brisbane,[7] who declares that the same world has yet to

<hr>

[6] [William Miller, founder of the sect of Millerites, who prophesied that the world would be destroyed in 1843.]

[7] [Albert Brisbane, the father of American Fourierism. Proposals for one of

begin, and waits a subscription of two hundred thousand dollars in order to start. Each man is free to present his notions on any subject. We have also talked, firm in the belief that the development of a nation's taste in art depends on a thousand deep-seated influences beyond the ken of the ignorant present; firm in the belief that freedom and knowledge will bear the fruit of refinement and beauty, we have yet dared to utter a few words of discontent, a few crude thoughts of what might be, and we feel the better for it. We promised ourselves nothing more than that satisfaction which Major Downing[8] attributes to every man "who has had his say, and then cleared out," and we already have a pleasant consciousness of what he meant by it.

---

his communal "Associations" called for public subscription to $400,000 of capital stock, half of which must be paid in cash.]

[8] [Major Downing was the pseudonym of Seba Smith, in his letters in Yankee dialect.]

Relative and Independent Beauty

HERE ARE THREADS OF relation which lead me from my specialty to the specialties of other men. Following this *commune quoddam vinculum,* I lay my artistic dogma at the feet of science; I test it by the traditional lore of handicraft; I seek a confirmation of these my inductions, or a contradiction and refutation of them; I utter these inductions as they occur to myself; I illustrate them by what they spontaneously suggest; I let them lead me as a child.

Persons whose light I have sought have been worried and fretted at the form, the body of my utterance. Since this soul, if soul it be, took the form of this body, I have received it as it came. If I seek another form, another dress than that with which my thought was born, shall I not disjoin that which is one? Shall I not disguise what I seek to decorate? I have seen that there is in the body and the dress an indication of the quantum and quality of the mind, and therefore doth it seem honest that I seek no other dress than mine own. I also know by heart some lines and proportions of the work of able penmen. The *lucidus ordo* of another mind is not displayed before me as pearls before swine. I love to bear in my bosom a nosegay plucked in classic ground: it sweetens me to myself. I respect too much the glory of Schiller and Winckelmann, of Goethe and Hegel, to dare purloin their vesture for my crudities. The partial development of my mind makes the dress and garb of imperfection proper for me. My notion of art is not a somewhat set forth for sale, that I should show it to advantage, or a soldier in uniform, anxious to pass muster, but rather a poor babe, whom I strip before the faculty, that they may counsel and advise— peradventure bid me despair.

Bodies are so varied by climate, and so changed by work, that it is rash to condemn them until impotence is demonstrated. The camelopard was long declared a monster, born of fancy, a nightmare of traveler's brain; but when the giraffe stood browsing in the treetops before us, we felt that we had been hasty. God's law is as far away from our taste as his ways are beyond our ways.

I know full well that, without dress and ornament, there are places whence one is expelled. I am too proud to seek admittance in disguise. I had rather remain in the street than get in by virtue of a borrowed coat. That which is partial and fractional may yet be sound and good as far as it goes.

In the hope that some persons, studious of art, may be curious to see how I develop the formula I have set up, I proceed. When I define Beauty as the promise of Function; Action as the presence of Function; Character as the record of Function, I arbitrarily divide that which is essentially one. I consider the phases through which organized intention passes to completeness, as if they were distinct entities. Beauty, being the promise of function, must be mainly present before the phase of action; but so long as there is yet a promise of function there is beauty, proportioned to its relation with action or with character. There is somewhat of character at the close of the first epoch of the organic life, as there is somewhat of beauty at the commencement of the last, but they are less apparent, and present rather to the reason than to sensuous tests.

If the normal development of organized life be from beauty to action, from action to character, the progress is a progress upward as well as forward; and action will be higher than beauty, even as the summer is higher than the spring; and character will be higher than action, even as autumn is the résumé and result of spring and summer. If this be true, the attempt to prolong the phase of beauty into the epoch of action can only be made through nonperformance; and false beauty or embellishment must be the result.

Why is the promise of function made sensuously pleasing? Because the inchoate organic life needs a care and protection beyond its present means of payment. In order that we may respect instinctive action, which is divine, are our eyes charmed by the aspect of infancy, and our hearts obedient to the command of a visible yet impotent volition.

The sensuous charm of promise is so great that the unripe reason seeks to make life a perennial promise; but promise, in the phase of action, receives a new name—that of nonperformance, and is visited with contempt.

The dignity of character is so great that the unripe reason seeks to mark the phase of action with the sensuous livery of character. The ivy is trained up the green wall, and while the promise is still fresh on every line of the building, its function is invaded by the ambition *to seem* to have lived.

Not to promise forever, or to boast at the outset, not to shine and to seem, but to be and to act, is the glory of any coördination of parts for an object.

I have spoken of embellishment as false beauty. I will briefly develop this view of embellishment. Man is an ideal being; standing, himself inchoate and incomplete, amid the concrete manifestations of nature, his first observation recognizes defect; his first action is an effort to complete his being. Not gifted, as the brutes, with an instinctive sense of completeness, he stands alone as capable of conative action. He studies himself; he disciplines himself.[1] Now, his best efforts at organization falling short of the need that is in his heart, and therefore infinite, he has sought to compensate for the defect in his plan by a charm of execution. Tasting sensuously the effect of a rhythm and harmony in God's world, beyond any adaptation of means to ends that his reason could measure and approve, he has sought to perfect his own approximation to the essential by crowning it with a wreath of measured

[1] [In his pseudonymous *Travels,* Greenough inserted here the exclamation, "Heautontimoroumenos!" (Self-torturer!)—the title of the play by Menander later adapted by Terence.]

73

and musical, yet nondemonstrable, adjunct. Now, I affirm that, from the ground whereon I stand and whence I think I see him operate, he thus mirrors, but darkly, God's world. By the sense of incompleteness in his plan, he shows the divine yearning that is in him; by the effort to compensate for defect in plan by any makeshift whatever, he forbids, or at least checks, further effort. I understand, therefore, by embellishment, THE INSTINCTIVE EFFORT OF INFANT CIVILIZATION TO DISGUISE ITS INCOMPLETENESS, EVEN AS GOD'S COMPLETENESS IS TO INFANT SCIENCE DISGUISED. The many-sided and full and rich harmony of nature is a many-sided response to the call for many functions; not an aesthetical utterance of the Godhead. In the tree and in the bird, in the shell and in the insect, we see the utterance of him who sayeth YEA, YEA, and NAY, NAY; and, therefore, whatever is assumed as neutral ground, or margin around the essential, will be found to come of evil, or, in other words, to be incomplete.

I base my opinion of embellishment upon the hypothesis that there is not one truth in religion, another in mathematics, and a third in physics and in art; but that there is one truth, even as one God, and that organization is his utterance. Now, organization obeys his law. It obeys his law by an approximation to the essential, and then there is what we term life; or it obeys his law by falling short of the essential, and then there is disorganization. I have not seen the inorganic attached to the organized but as a symptom of imperfect plan, or of impeded function, or of extinct action.

The normal development of beauty is through action to completeness. The invariable development of embellishment and decoration is more embellishment and more decoration. The *reductio ad absurdum* is palpable enough at last; but where was the first downward step? I maintain that the first downward step was *the introduction of the first inorganic, nonfunctional element, whether of shape or color.* If I be told that such a system as mine would produce *nakedness,* I accept the omen. In nakedness I behold the majesty of the essential instead of the trappings of pretension. The agendum is not diminished; it is infinitely extended. We shall have grasped with tiny hands the standard of Christ, and borne it into the academy, when we shall call upon the architect, and sculptor, and painter to seek to be perfect even as our Father is perfect. The assertion that the human body is other than a fit exponent and symbol of the human being is a falsehood, I believe. I believe it to be false on account of the numerous palpable falsehoods which have been necessary in order to clinch it.

Beauty is the promise of Function. Solomon in all his glory is, therefore, not arrayed as the lily of the field. Solomon's array is the result of the instinctive effort of incompleteness to pass itself for complete. It is pretension. When Solomon shall have appreciated nature and himself, he will reduce his household, and adapt his harness, not for pretension, but for performance. The lily is arrayed in heavenly beauty because it is organized, both in shape and color, to dose the germ of future lilies with atmospheric and solar influence.

We now approach the grand conservative trap, the basis of independent beauty. Finding in God's world a sensuous beauty not organically demonstrated to us, the hierarchies call on us to shut our eyes and kneel to an aesthetical utterance of the divinity. I refuse. Finding here an apparent embellishment, I consider the appearance of embellishment an accusation of ignorance and incompleteness in my science. I confirm my refusal after recalling the fact that science has thus far done nothing else than resolve the lovely on the one hand, the hateful on the other, into utterances of the Godhead—the former being yea, the latter nay. As the good citizen obeys the good law because it is good, and the bad law that its incompleteness be manifest, so does every wrong result from divine elements, accuse the organization, and by pain and woe represent X, or the desired solution. To assert that this or that form or color is beautiful *per se* is to formulate prematurely; it is to arrogate godship; and once that false step is taken, human-godship or tyranny is inevitable without a change of creed.

The first lispings of science declared that nature abhors a vacuum; there we see humanity expressing its ignorance by transferring a dark passion to the Godhead which is light and love. This formula could not outlive experiment, which has demonstrated that God's care upholds us with so many pounds to the square inch of pressure on every side, and that the support is variable. The ancients knew somewhat of steam. They formulated steam as a devil. The vessels at Pompeii all speak one language—look out for steam! The moderns have looked into steam, and, by wrestling with him, have forced him to own himself an angel—an utterance of love and care.

We are told that we shall know trees by their fruits: even because of the fruits of refusing to kneel, and of worshiping with the eyes open, do I proceed to seek that I may find.

Mr. Garbett, in his learned and able treatise on the principles of design in architecture,[2] has dissected the English house and found with the light of two words, fallen from Mr. Emerson, the secret of the inherent ugliness of that structure. It is the *cruelty* and *selfishness* of a London house, he says (and I think he proves it, too), which affects us so disagreeably as we look upon it. Now, these qualities in a house, like the blear-eyed stolidity of a habitual sot, are symptoms, not diseases. Mr. Garbett should see herein the marvelous expression of which bricks and mortar can be made the vehicles. In vain will he attempt to get by embellishment a denial of selfishness, so long as selfishness reigns. To medicate symptoms will never, at best, do more than effect a metastasis—suppress an eruption; let us believe, rather, that the Englishman's love of home has expelled the selfishness from the boudoir, the kitchen, and the parlor, nobler organs, and thrown it out on the skin, the exterior, where it less threatens life, and stands only for X, or a desired solution. If I have been clear in what I have said, it will be apparent that the intention, the soul of an organization, will

[2] [Edward Lacy Garbett, *Rudimentary Treatise on the Principles of Design in Architecture as Deducible from Nature and Exemplified in the Works of the Greek and Gothic Architects* (London, J. Weale, 1850), a once popular volume, No. 18 in Weale's "Rudimentary" series.]

get utterance in the organization in proportion to the means at its disposal: in vain shall you drill the most supple body of him that hates me into a manifestation of love for me; while my blind and deaf cousin will soon make me feel, and pleasingly feel, that I was the man in all the world that he wished to meet.

In seeking, through artistic analysis, a confirmation of my belief in one God, I offend such hierarchies as maintain that there be two Gods: the one good and *all*-powerful, the other evil and somewhat powerful. It is only necessary, in order to demolish the entire structure I have raised, that some advocate of independent beauty and believer in the devil—for they go and come together—demonstrate embellishment for the sake of beauty in a work of the divine hand. Let me be understood; I cannot accept as a demonstration of embellishment a sensuous beauty not yet organically explained. I throw the *onus probandi* on him who commands me to kneel. I learned this trick in Italy, where the disappointed picture dealer often defied me, denying his daub to be a Raphael, to say, then, what it was. No, my friend, I care not whose it is; when I say certainly not a Raphael, I merely mean that I will none of it.

If there be in religion any truth, in morals any beauty, in art any charm, but through fruits, then let them be demonstrated; and the demonstration, in regard to morals and faith, will work backward and enlighten art.

I have diligently sought, with scalpel and pencil, an embellishment for the sake of beauty, a sacrifice of function to other than destruction. I have not found it. When I, therefore, defy the believer in the devil to show me such an embellishment, I do so humbly. I want help.

It seems to me that a word of caution is necessary before seeking independent beauty. Beauty may be present, yet not be recognized as such. If we lack the sense of the promise of function, beauty for us will not exist. The inhabitants of certain Swiss valleys regard a goiter as ornamental. It is somewhat superadded to the essential, and they see it under the charm of association. The courtiers of Louis XIV admired the *talon rouge* and the enormous *perruque*. They were somewhat superadded to the essential, and they saw them under the charm of association. But the educated anatomist in Switzerland sees the goiter as we see it. The educated artist of Louis XIV's time saw the maiming pretension of his dress as we see it.

The aim of the artist, therefore, should be first to seek the essential; when the essential hath been found, then, if ever, will be the time to commence embellishment.[3] I will venture to predict that the essential, when found, will be complete. I will venture to predict that completeness will instantly throw off all that is not itself, and will thus command: "Thou shalt have no other Gods beside me." In a word, completeness is the absolute utterance of the Godhead; not the completeness of the Catholic bigot, or of the Quaker, which is a pretended one, obtained by negation of God-given tendencies; but the completeness of the sea, which hath a smile as unspeakable as the darkness of its wrath; the completeness of earth, whose every atom is a microcosm; the completeness of the human body, where all relations are resumed at once and dominated. As the monarch rises out of savage manhood a plumed

[3] [As any book is entitled to a digression, let one be made here. Boswell's *Johnson* supplies the matter: "We then fell into a disquisition whether there is any beauty independent of utility. The General (Paoli) maintained there was not. Dr. Johnson maintained that there was; and he instanced a coffee cup which he held in his hand, the painting of which was of no real use, as the cup would hold the coffee equally well if plain; yet the painting was beautiful." The Great Cham's logic was tangential, that time, and the "disquisition" never did return to the point; but later he veered a little nearer to what Greenough was to get at: "Johnson expressed his disapprobation of ornamental architecture . . . 'because it consumes labor disproportionate to its utility'. For the same reason he satirised statuary. . . . 'What, sir' (said Mr. Gwyn, the architect), 'will you allow no value to beauty in architecture or in statuary? Why should we allow it, then, in writing? Why do you take the trouble to give us so many fine allusions, and bright images, and elegant phrases? You might convey all your instruction without these ornaments.' Johnson smiled with complacency; but said, 'Why, sir, all these ornaments are useful, because they obtain an easier reception for truth; but a building is not at all more convenient for being decorated with superfluous carved work.' "]

czar, embellishing his shortcomings with the sensuous livery of promise, yet, entering the phase of developed thought and conscious vigor, stands the eagle-eyed and gray-coated Bonaparte, so will every development of real humanity pass through the phase of nondemonstrable embellishment, which is a false completeness, to the multiform organization which responds to every call.

I hold the human body, therefore, to be a multiform command. Its capacities are the law and gauge of manhood as connected with earth. I hold the blessings attendant upon obedience to this command to be the yea, yea; the woe consequent upon disobedience, the nay, nay, of the Godhead. These God daily speaketh to him whose eyes and ears are open. Other than these I have not heard. When, therefore, the life of man shall have been made to respond to the command which is in his being, giving the catholic result of a sound collective mind in a sound aggregate body, he will organize his human instrument or art for its human purpose, even as he shall have adapted his human life to the divine instrument which was given him. I wish to be clear; the instrument or body being of divine origin, we formulate rashly when we forego it before thoroughly responding to its requirement. That it is in itself no final or complete entity is herein manifest, that it changes. The significance of yesterday, today, and tomorrow is this, that we are in a state of development. Now, the idea of development necessarily supposes incompleteness; now, completeness can know no change. The instrument of body is no haphazard datum, given as an approximation, whose shortcomings we are to correct by convention, arbitrium, and whim, but an absolute requirement, and only then responding to the divine intention when its higher nature shall be unfolded by high function, even as the completeness of the brute responds to the requirement of his lower nature.

Internecine war is the law of brute existence. War! The lion lives not by food alone. Behold, how he pines and dwindles as he growls over his butcher's meat! It is in the stealthy march, the ferocious bound, and deadly grapple, tearing palpitating flesh from writhing bone—a halo of red rain around his head—that he finds the completion of his being, in obedience to a word that proceeded out of the mouth of God. Now, the law of brute life is the law of human life, in so far as the brute man is undeveloped in his higher tendencies. They, therefore, who, having formulated a credo for infant intelligence, and finding domination thereby secured, proceed to organize a *perennial infancy,* that they may enjoy an eternal dominion, will sooner or later see their sheep transformed to tigers; for the law of development, being a divine law, can only be withstood by perishing. If what I have said be true, collective manhood will never allow exceptional development to slumber at the helm or to abuse the whip. Collective manhood calls for development. If exceptional development answer—Lo! ye are but wolves, manhood will reply—Then, have at you! He who cannot guide must come down. We feel that we cannot remain where we are.

I have followed the train of remark whither it led me. Let us resume. Organization being the passage of intention through function to completeness, the expressions of its phases are symptoms only. The same philosophy which has cloaked, and crippled, and smothered the human body as rebelling against its Creator, yet always in vain, because the human body, like the Greek hero, says, Strike! but learn,—that philosophy has set up a theory of beauty by authority, of beauty independent of other things than its own mysterious harmony with the human soul. Thus, we remark that the human soul, so inclined to evil in the moral world, according to the same philosophy, is sovereign arbiter of beauty in the aesthetical world. The Creator, who formed man's soul with a thirst for sin, and his body as a temple of shame, has, therefore, made his taste infallible! Let us seek through the whole history of arbitrary embellishment to find a resting-place. We shall look in vain; for the introduction of the inorganic into the organized is destruction; its development has ever been a *reductio ad absurdum*.

There is no conceivable function which does not obey an absolute law. The approximation to that law in material, in parts, in their form, color, and relations, is the measure of freedom or obedience to God, in life. The attempt to stamp the green fruit, the dawning science, the inchoate life, as final, by such exceptional minds and social achievements as have produced a wish to remain here, and a call for a tabernacle, *these are attempts to divide manhood, which is one;* they are attempts to swim away from brute man, sinking in the sea of fate. They will ever be put to shame; for the ignorance of the ignorant confounds the wise; for the filth of the filthy befouls the clean; for the poverty of the poor poisons the quiet of the possessor. The brute man clings to the higher man; he loves him even as himself; he cannot be shaken off; he must be assimilated and absorbed.

I call therefore upon science in all its branches to arrest the tide of sensuous and arbitrary embellishment, so far as it can do it, not negatively by criticism thereof alone, but positively by making the instrument a many-sided response to the multiform demands of life. The craving for completeness will then obtain its normal food in results, not the opiate and deadening stimulus of decoration. Then will structure and its dependent sister arts emerge from the standstill of *ipse dixit* and, like the ship, the team, the steam engine, proceed through phases of development toward a response to need.

The truth of such doctrine, if truth be in it, must share the fate of other truth, and offend him whose creed is identified with the false; it must meet the indifference of the many who believe that a new truth is born every week for him who can afford to advertise. But it must earn a place in the heart of him who has sought partial truths with success; for truths are all related.

Burke on the Beautiful

BURKE HAS DEVELOPED, at length, the negative examination of beauty. He arrives at no result by this course, because negative analysis can only attain its object by exhausting negation; which is not possible in this vast field of inquiry.

When at last he affirms, he says roundly that Beauty is a positive entity, cognizable by the sense. He proceeds to enumerate the qualities which, he thinks, constitute beauty in visible objects. He states these as follows: Smallness, Smoothness, Gradual Variation, Delicacy, Color.

Smallness.—One may well be startled at the list of positive entities which commences with size, for which, even in trade, we have only an approximative standard. The pendulum which beats seconds in a given latitude must share the imperfection of the measure of time; it must feel, more or less, the variation of temperature in its dimension. The bare element of size explains to me the grandeur of the alp and the elephant, the endearing dependence of the babe, and the attraction of the hummingbird; but the significance of dimension in all these cases, and in every case that I conceive, is a relative significance. When Burke found the sense of the sublime to result alike from the contemplation of the orbs that roll in space, and the idea of beings that elude the test of the microscope, I must think that he should have concluded that the sublime is no quality in things, having a positive existence, but a *mental perception* of *relation*.

Smoothness.—This, again, is a relative quality. The smoothness of the teeth, and of a marble or porphyry table, is one; the smoothness of the eyeball, the brow, the cheek is another. If anyone doubt the organic significance of smoothness, let him imagine the smoothness of the teeth transferred to the lip, that of the eyeball to the eyelid, that of the varnished bud of April to the petal of the rose in June, that of the billiard ball to the hand of the maiden. Smoothness is mere negation. The smoothness of the eyeball is on the one hand a ball-and-socket smoothness like that of the head of the femur and the acetabulum, a lubricated smoothness. It is on the other hand a crystalline smoothness, related to the function of transmitting light and color. The smoothness of cutlery, as it comes from the hand of the artisan, is an organic smoothness. The perfection of the polish proclaims the entireness of the promise. It begins to lose that polish as soon as its action commences, and at last retains mainly the beauty of form. If anyone doubt that the perception of smoothness is a relative perception, let him, for one minute, rub the palms of his hands upon sandstone, and then rub them together.

Gradual variation.—Variation is characteristic of organic rhythm, whether in the works of nature or those of man; but the perception of gradation is the perception of relation, whether the gradation be one of size, or of form, or of tint. To prove gradation a positive element of beauty, it would be necessary to show that the greater the gradation, or the greater the variety of gradation, the greater would be the beauty, an assertion to be easily estimated after a glance at the human eye.

Delicacy.—By delicacy, as an element of beauty, Burke is careful to tell us that he does not mean weakness, or any modification in the direction of weakness, but only the absence of roughness and excessive robustness. Now, it is not apparent that he means anything more, by this quality, than a normal and healthy apportionment of means to ends; if he does, then has he foisted into the academy the taste of the boudoir and the drawing room, which can only earn respect *there* as a pupil. His delicacy in such case must share the fate of Hogarth's "*grandeur* of the *periwig*," and be the creature of convention—ridiculous, except in the time, place, and circumstances that gave its value.

If you can establish the opinion that ladies should hobble about with difficulty, the crippled foot would please our eyes, as it is said to charm those of the mandarin. If you can prove that the human hand was intended as a proclamation of idleness and effeminacy, the nauseous claws seen in the East, and sometimes cultivated by persons in civilized countries, will have a suggestive charm.

Color.—That the modifications of light have an organic significance and are not positive elements of beauty, results to my mind from the fact that there is a degree of light which surfeits, a want of it which starves the visual organ. The absence of color in the teeth is as beautiful as its presence in the lips. The contrast of the two heightens each, and exemplifies a charm where gradual variation has no place. Now its absence in the one case and the presence in the other has an organic and functional import and meaning. The dark polish of ice and the pure white of snow are alike mechanical defenses of the permanence of these forms of water.

I think it of the highest importance that we continue the investigation of the functional significance of color rather than close the school with an anodyne formula, because whether the eye be adapted to objects in nature, or these to the eye, true it is that the relation is a vital one. I will be rash enough to confess that I have an instinctive belief that the eye is, under God, the creature of the sun; for I find it made in his own image, and I seek it in vain in such fishes, for instance, as know him not.

In order to prove that beauty consists of positive elements cognizable by the sense, I think it must be shown that the beauty is *in proportion* to the *presence* of the elements, and that where these elements are *diminished* or suppressed for the sake of function, beauty shall be diminished in proportion to their *absence*. Now this may be done to the satisfaction of the milliner or the "petite maîtresse," but never to the satisfaction of the philosopher or the artist.

Burke was bold when he invited the world to a feast of beauty with so meager a bill of fare. With the exception of delicacy, by which I know not what he means, in philosophy, I believe that all the other elements he has mentioned can be exemplified and even combined into the most sickening manifestation of morbid action. Skin disease and imposthume will display them all, and force the student to go farther for the secret of beauty, even at the risk of faring worse.

It is natural to suppose that the soul of any civilization will find utterance in its statement of what its *love* is and should be. Have not theories of beauty been invented to fit "spoon-fashion" certain systems of politics and morals? Is it not from an unconscious desire to *constitute* and *limit* the *good* that we seek the good with such starveling formulas? I believe the beautiful to be the promise and announcement of the good; to seek the semblance thereof, rather than the true, has been, is, and must be the occupation of such as seek the beautiful only in pursuit of the good.

He who seeks the beautiful in the stupendous system of nature will seek in vain for a positive entity whose elements, cognizable by sense, can be set down like the ingredients of a dish or the inventory of a portmanteau. I doubt if he ever find anything more tan-

gible than the human soul; if he does, I will venture
to predict that it will be somewhat more than small,
smooth, gradually varied, delicate, and of pleasing
color.

To the generality of men the sight of a skull,
whether of man or beast, is rather painful. They view
it in relation to disorganization, of which we all have
an instinctive horror. Why, then, to the anatomist and
the artist is the skull a beautiful, a sublime object? Because they have minutely investigated its relation to
life. All its forms, surfaces, and dimensions speak of
its former contents, vesture, and capacities. That pale
spheroidal dome is a model of the globe, those lack-
luster eyeless holes beneath, speak of the heavens; they
echo the distant sun.

Why, in the crowded thoroughfare, do we pass nine
men in ten without emotion and as if they were not?
Why are we so patiently incurious respecting the myriads of human beings who have laid the basis of our
actual being? Why in the first sight of a foreign city,
whose language is as unknown to us as its streets, does
the heart shrink back on itself? Why, in such position,
does the coin in our pockets assume an importance
unfelt before? In all cases because of relation. This it is
that makes the Austrian prince spurn, as less than

man, all beneath the barons.[1] This it is which melts the divine Savior into tenderness at the sight of sin and sorrow. The positive sound of cannon is not much; it is relation that makes the growl of the morning gun at Gibraltar the voice of the British lion, and, therefore, does the responsive thunder of Ceuta sound a good-morrow from the African shore. When, in the breathless court, the word "guilty" drops from the lips of the foreman, why does it ring satisfaction to the ear of the stern attorney, and for the prisoner at the bar strike the larum of despair? It is the relative import of things that characterizes their perception, and that with which we have no relation, for us is not.

With what positive result do we, then, close this review of Mr. Burke's position? With a conviction which, if it be well grounded, is not only of artistic but of general importance. In a world of dependence and of relation to a being like man, whose isolated mind collapses to idiocy, whose isolated body is the slave of its lower want, that which is fitted to one relation is therefore *unfitted* for another and different relation. That which is beautiful in one connection is *therefore* deformed in another and different connection. To deal with relative elements as if they were positive is to in-

---

[1] Der Mensch fængt mit dem Baron an.—Dictum of Windischgrätz.

sure discord and disorganization—for as the charm of rhyme resides not in "dove" or "love," but in the perception of the dependence of sound,—as the charm of verse lies not in its positive structure, but in the relation it bears to the thought, and the breath that makes it heard,—so has all that sways the mind, the heart, the sense of man, only a relative and dependent being.

The entire gamut of visual qualities in objects is, therefore, a language, a tongue, whose vocabulary must be learned, word by word, and which has already been mastered to an extent that justifies the surmise, that its elements have force from their relation, and not from positive existence; since God alone truly is.

Criticism in Search of Beauty

To MANY MINDS THE definition of Beauty as the promise of Function must appear an excessive generalization. To many minds such expanse dilutes all substances and leaves but their air as a result. Yet is this generalization but an effort to grasp a wider collection of phenomena, and, if developed, it is not certain that it will prove other than a step to a wider and a higher generalization.

Hogarth's ingenious plea for his line of beauty holds good with regard to the spinal column and the necks of long-necked birds and beasts. It is the line of moving water, of flowing draperies, and of many pleasing vegetable forms; but if we drop from the flank of the horse, where we find it, to the shank, which is thin, straight, and hard, we get a new sense of beauty, and not a sacrifice thereof. With Hogarth's formula in hand, we must accept the vagaries of Bernini and condemn the Greek peristyle and pediment. This famed line is truly indicative of motion, of the double element of inertia or resistance on the one hand and of a moving power on the other. From its inevitable significance and uniformity of expression it becomes monotonous by repetition, incongruous and impertinent wherever such double action is out of place. Transfer the waving line of a horse's flank to his metatarsal bone, and you have a cripple. Transfer the double curve of a swan's neck to his bell, and you have an impotent and therefore ridiculous arrangement.

The right line is perhaps susceptible of more various significance than any other line whatever. The right line vertical, as seen in the pendent chain, is indicative of utter flexibility; in the staff whose base is buried, of stark rigidity. Horizontal, it proclaims equal support throughout its length, whether from its own consistence or from extraneous prop. Inclined, it declares a double thrust in opposite directions. Observe the folds of linen that drop, like organ pipes, from the girdle of Pallas; transfer your eye to yonder spear on which Adonis leans; remark how nearly identical are the forms, how directly reversed is the expression of these cylindrical shapes! Such forms have therefore a *force* and a *speech* analogous to the virtues of the vocabulary. Their significance is relative and dependent. They may not be safely used as positive entities.

Let us dwell for a moment upon one of the chief means of embellishment, the adoption of the sequence and rhythm of organization, as an aesthetical element of positive import, apart from all requirement *save the craving of the eye*. The leaf, the flower, the chain, the contorted spiral of the cable, the alternations of the woven withe of the basket, have, among other similar functional arrangements, been pressed into the service of the decorator to fill that vacuum which the heart of man abhors. The eye responds inevitably to the sensuous charm and the associated expression of these forms; but if we reflect deeply on the source of this gratification we shall detect their real character. Thus enjoyed, this rhythm is never truly generative; for if the organizations they were intended to complete had *no requirement* of their *own*, whose spaces and means have been *usurped* by their quotations, then I affirm that these extraneous and irrelevant forms invade that *silence* which alone is worthy of man when there is nothing to be said. To my sense, therefore, these forms

99

only accuse a vacuum. They accuse it credibly, and the eye assents to them; but though they *accuse* they do not *fill* it, since the more we get of them the more we ask, until performance reels and slavery dies, under the requirement. Such is the result of dealing with the relative and finite as if it were a positive, a divine being.

What is the real meaning of that vast aggregation of marble and gilding—of silks and jewels, of glass and metal, of carved and painted embellishment which is called St. Peter's church? Throwing and holding aloft the gilded symbol of self-sacrifice and love to man, whose glimmer flashes on the one hand to the gulf of Genova, on the other to the waves of the Adriatic, is it not a giant's attempt to scale the heavens?—the affirmation of the positive in the relative—a mechanical assertion of spirit—an attempt at arithmetical demonstration that Christ's kingdom *is* of this world? When, amid the gorgeous retinue of bedizened prelates, the triple-crowned Pontiff, crippled by weight of frippery, is borne on subject shoulders to that balcony, when the peacocks' tails are waved about his head, and he utters his presumptuous blessing, "Urbi et Orbi,"—while kneeling troops clash their weapons as they go down, and trumpets laugh and cannons thunder from the fortress of the Holy Angel;—when the sense and the imagination is thus appealed to in base assertion, what is the practical result? What are the *fruits* by which alone this tree must at last be judged? The perfumed sweetness of that vast pile hath cured no yellow and swollen victim of Pontine miasma. The weight of that expenditure hath crushed to earth the denizens of the patrimony of St. Peter, since Mary must daily bring the precious ointment for a Christ who is always with us and whose wordly pomp outvies the arrogance of kings. For each effeminate warbling of soprano Latin praise to God in the temple, there go up a thousand curses of tyrants, in the vernacular, from the thorough-fare, the hovel, and the dungeon. When was the absolute other than the paramour of the expedient? . . .

To what, at length, is the size of St. Peter's church related? Is it a lodging for prayer? Christ has recommended a closet. Is it to receive the laity of the earth? All earth is a temple to him who looks upward, and naught less will suffice for man. The size of St. Peter's church is, therefore, a pretension. It affirms of the tree its roots, its soil, and its branches; and these it measures. As a result of nearly two thousand years' preaching of the doctrine of self-sacrifice and the laying up of treasure in Heaven it is a *reductio ad absurdum*.

Criticism has shaped another theory of Beauty. The beautiful has been defined as a result of the combination of Uniformity with Variety. This combination is indeed universally found in organization, whether in the works of nature or of man; but the theory asserts too much, since, if true, beauty can be produced by mere mechanical means, and England would make it with steam power, and flood the globe therewith. This theory is sustained in the hope of divorcing the beautiful and the good. It is sustained in the hope of giving the former and receiving the latter. The sensuous adjunct of intention, when divorced from that intention, loses at once its virtue, and retains its charm only so long as its emptiness is unsuspected. The smile of benevolence may be assumed also, and may pass currently with the world, but if too many practice this beautiful art, frowns will at last come to be in fashion.

When Homer would give us the idea of womanly charm in Helen, he seeks no positive ingredients to wake our enthusiasm. He makes the princess to pass through a crowd of aged men, who are reviling her as the cause of their woe, and at her aspect they are hushed in mute admiration. When she has passed away, they swear with one accord that such a vision is worth the ten years' war, and the burning of the ships and the slaughter of the men. Achilles, who remains in every scholar's mind the type of manly beauty, is painted as swift of foot and the most beautiful of all the Greeks who went to Troy. These beauties, then, have been created by relation in our own minds, and we have done the work with the bard; and it is because that work is a delight that we love him. If criticism had other than a negative power, we might reproduce the phenomena of a Shakespeare or a Dante. It is because the speech of these men is inalienably *theirs,* related more to themselves than to the positive, that we may hope to approach the latter rather than to repeat them.

The creation of beauty in art, as in other forms of poetry, is a welling up from the depths of the soul, not a scientific synthesis. There has been in England, since 1815, more discussion of aesthetical doctrine, more analysis, experiment, and dogged determination to effect somewhat in art, than attended the birth of the Florentine school; but always in the main impotent, because the governing intellect of England has held art to be a *thing,* a plant growing by human knowledge, with gold for its nutriment. Art is not a thing, but a form, a development of man—"La vostra Arte quasi di Dio e nipote." The artistic power, whatever it be, has no positive existence. Like the organ in our churches, on weekdays, it stands dumb and dead till the constituency drive through its pipes the health of life and minister to its requirement.

I will seek to make clearer what I have said by a rapid glance at the career of pictorial art. In the great works of the Roman and Florentine schools we behold the highest development of thought and feeling in the pictorial form. These great masters always based their creations upon tangible, palpable, everyday truth. The mother bears her babe, the Savior embraces his cross. The heavens, as they open, reflect earth, and worship the Deity with words of human speech. Titian, in his color, is not less true to the concrete. As art declined, we find the process to be one of separating the sensuously pleasing from its organic relation; till, in Luca Giordano and Boucher, we find a chaos of bombast, falsehood, and clogging sensuality. This farrago corrupted still further the appetite that demanded it, and Boucher had for a successor a worse than Boucher, till utter impotence gave at length silence and repose.

There is a sensation analogous to the sense of beauty, which is effected somewhat independent of function, nay, running oftentimes counter to the requirement of function. This is the offspring of the fashion, the mode, omnipotent for an hour, contemptible when that hour is passed. I have yet to see any solid reason for receiving nine-tenths of the architectural features of our actual structures as other than a servile obeisance to this despotic requirement from abroad. He whose eye is tickled by the play of light and shadow, and the merely picturesque projections of the present fashion, will be inclined to flout me when I hint that these are a jargon and no tongue. Their features, which seem of such significance, will, however, inevitably turn out at last, like the cant phrases of the rabble, to mean whatever you please, merely because they mean nothing. Once adopt the principles by which alone they can be defended, and there is no bar between you and the prolific silliness of Borromini, excepting the want of funds. These feats have effected what I once believed impossible; they have made the sober and the true enamored of the old, bald, neutral-toned, Yankee farmhouse which seems to belong to the ground whereon it stands, as the caterpillar to the leaf that feeds him.

The expression of life, which is what we all crave, can only be obtained by *living*. I have seen a clergyman of the established church who long appeared to me an overgrown automaton in which the digestive apparatus was exaggerated. He was an incarnation of vicarious being. He seemed to have been taken into the world and *done for.* Inoffensive was he—well-begotten and respectable; for he had been educated among scholars—dressed by a tailor, and dressed well—shaved by a barber, and well shorn—insured by a solvent company here below—saved by his Savior in the world to come, so that one saw no obstacle to his translation to another sphere except his weight. Yet was all this only apparent, for no sooner was a trout stream mentioned than the kaleidoscope revolved, the fog rolled from before his eyes, and he became animated and alert. There was, after all, an agendum. Now it is clear that this man was a crushed individuality, born out of time or place. Like the potato which has sprouted in the crypt, this poor soul had sent its pale elongated shoot through darkness and prohibition till it found the light and air of freedom at a cranny, when it instantly assumed its color, threw out its leaves, and *was*—a human otter.

If it were true that the sense of beauty in nature and in art finds its nourishment in the *pleasing,* independent of other than its *own relation* to the innate craving of man; if it were true that beauty is a *tertium quid* thrown into ingredients in themselves indifferent, to fill a psychological vacuum, as salt and sugar are added to compounds which offend through acid or pall by insipidity, then should we behold professors of beauty

who would translate into the vulgar tongue what
Mahomet meant by his houris, what the Northmen
meant by drinking beer in skulls, what the Indian
meant by his happy hunting grounds, what the Christian preacher means by that which "eye hath not seen
nor ear heard." The man possessed of this catholicon
would be able to adorn and sanctify the humblest, the
most repulsive details of life. These details are, in fact,
adorned and sanctified to man—not by any combination of uniformity with variety, or waving line, or other
like futile mechanical grasp at the unspeakable, but by
their RELATION to *"things hoped for."*

The men who in Greece and Italy earned a remem-
brance as creators of the beautiful were most untiring
students of organization, of the relations of anteced-
ence and consequence. More has been said about the
art of pleasing by ingenious Englishmen and Frenchmen than can be found in all the disquisitions of
Leonardo, or Leon Battista Alberti, or Raffaello. How
does he of Urbino, who has held the world captive, define the beautiful which was his magic scepter? He
says, in plain words, that is was a "certa idea che ho
nella mente"—a certain idea that I have in my mind.

The skillful analysis of the relations of color and
sound in their modifications to the rhythm of organi-

zation, tending without doubt to assist our conception of all related things, is but the servant and never the master of creative mind. Dealing with such elements only as the reason has incarnated in propositions, they have in that incarnation dropped all divinity, which is unspeakable, and have taken their humble place among things. Such results are but the *record* of a mental, as the footprint of man is the record of a physical function, proclaiming, it is true, the beauty of the related parts which achieved the step, but impotent as a creative power. As well may you hope to beget eloquence of pure grammar, as music of science, or beauty of things.

Organization and dissolution: these are the two poles of the divine magnet, and to the pure intelligence the one is as harmonious a speech as the other, since it is its correlative. That the sense revolts at the phenomena of disorganization proves only the relation of the body to things; but that relation being a divine datum, the marriage of the sensuous phenomena of life to the action of decay cannot be other than poisonous and suicidal.

Is the display which has lantern-led princes and people other than a rhythm of disorganization sensuously enjoyed because its functional significance was not apparent? If the moral and political phenomena attendant upon vigorous attempts after beauty, independent of function, had not been constant and unvarying, I should doubt any mental induction that accused such import in adornment. Luxury and decay have not been separated, and the only terms on which both can be long kept up is to regard the crucified *homo* as a symbol of collective man made the groveling basis of exceptional development and well-being.

Whence is derived the attraction of the playhouse and the opera? I believe that these fruits of civilization are pleasing, but, to the mass, sensuous special pleadings against the dogma which, condemning the body, commands us to perish. Feeling a void in our hearts, amid the negative requirements of the lawgiver and the priest, we ask the spectacle at least of untrammeled life, and hire the dancing girl to give a vicarious grace and joy, driven from among us by a sour and one-sided dogma. Now, it will be apparent to reflection and to the heart that the dancing girl is degraded by representing a fraction of humanity. The greater her beauty, the more perfect the response of her limbs and the vivacity of her foot to the joyous notes of the composer, the greater the degradation. That divine instrument before us *is* the representative of womanhood, and *is* degraded by aught less than true woman's life. Not with impunity, therefore, shall we gaze upon her in that monstrous relation, for, though we may forget it, yet is she nevertheless our sister. There is here a sin, and a grievous sin—not in the light of that eye that flashes, not in the music of that frame that takes captive the sense, not in the panting of that perhaps virgin bosom, but in the hireling divorce of these phenomena from their normal and organic sequence in human life. *There* lies the prostitution—there the selfishness and the vice, and therefore the destruction.

The East Indian bigot who seeks to please God by maintaining one posture till the articulations have stiffened him to a monument of monomania, and the paid exponent of youthful joy and desire—these are extreme expressions of a prohibition to live. As the one kills by checking function, so the other destroys by the inculcation of vicarious life. I will close this statement by an affirmation which formerly could not have been spoken without perishing in the flames; and which, even now, cannot perhaps be spoken with impunity. That which the human being was made to bear, the human being was not made to bear the want of.

To follow blindly the dictates of sense and instinctive craving, *that* is to be a brute and not a man; to deny the promptings of sense and instinctive craving, *that* is to perish. Behold the absolute. Between these lies human life, an existence for which no revelation will ever afford a mechanical rule or absolute dogma without its immediate translation from time to eternity; for to seek the true, *this* is truly to live in time—which only is, through succession of phenomena, to find it,—*this* will be to repose in the bosom of omniscience; for where all is absolutely right nothing can change, since truth is not a series of approximations but an arrival and a result.

Therefore do I feel that this American people is the advanced guard of humanity; because it is one vast interrogation. Never affirming but when there is need of action, in its affirmation conceding that the minority represents a sacred human want not yet articulate to the aggregate ear, it gives peace and good will in proportion to the universality of the wants to which it ministers. If the passion displayed in the alternation of hope and fear fright the timid and skeptical, the lull of the storm, when the sovereignty has spoken, is full of hope for a distant futurity, for it proves that our political constitution, like the human frame, is not less wonderfully than fearfully made.

III

Structure and Organization

I T IS USELESS TO REGRET that discussions of principle involve, to a certain extent, persons also. If this were not, on the whole, a good arrangement, principles would have been furnished with a better lodging. I take it that passions and interests are the great movers and steadiers of the social world, and that principles, like the bread on Sir John Falstaff's score, are an unconscionably small item.

The working forces and restraints are, like the furnaces and engines, the lock up and lock out of the mint at Philadelphia, all very effective for their objects. A showy front masks all these things and adorns Chestnut Street by the maimed quotation of a passage of Greek eloquence relating to something else. A huge brick chimney rising in the rear talks English and warns you that the façade is to be taken with some grains of allowance.

The domain of taste is eminently one of free discussion. In most civilized countries the individual is restrained by the magistracy from offending the public eye by unsightly or ill-timed exhibitions of any very peculiar dogma of his own, because it is thought that the harm thus done to the public is not compensated by the gratification of the unit. Still, he is allowed to maintain his theory by any means short of an invasion of the public sense of propriety.

One unaccustomed to trace the influence of associated ideas, of example, and of authority, would naturally suppose that each climate, each creed and form of government, would stamp its character readily and indelibly upon the structures of a thinking population. It is not so. It is only by degrees that leisure and wealth find means to adapt forms, elsewhere invented, to new situations and new wants.

When civilization gradually develops an indigenous type, the complex result still carries the visible germ whence it sprang. The harmony of the Chinese structures indicates a oneness of origin and modification. The sign manual of the Sultan is but the old mark pompously flourished. There is a blood relationship between the pipe of the North American savage and the temples of Central America.

In the architecture of Greece, of Italy, and of the more recent civilizations, on the other hand, we remark a struggle between an indigenous type, born of the soil and of the earlier wants of a people, and an imported theory which, standing upon a higher artistic ground, captivates the eye and wins the approval of dawning taste. If my limits permitted, it were not amiss to trace this conquest of refinement, and to follow it out also in relation to literature, and to dress, and amusements. The least effort of memory will suggest numerous invasions of artistic theory upon primitive expedients, conflicts between the home-grown habit which has possession and exotic theory which seeks it.

There is one feature in all the great developments of architecture which is worthy to occupy us for a moment. They are all fruits of a dominating creed. If we consider how vast was the outlay they required, we shall not wonder that religion alone has thus far been able to unite, in a manner to wield them, the motives and the means for grand and consistent systems of structure. The magnificence of the Romans, the splendor of Venice and Genoa, like the ambitious efforts of

France, England, and Germany in more recent days, had a certain taint of dilettantism in their origin, which, aiming to combine inconsistent qualities, and that for a comparatively low motive, carried through all their happiest combinations the original sin of impotence, and gave, as a result, bombast instead of eloquence, fritter instead of richness, baldness for simplicity, carving in lieu of sculpture. The laws of expression are such that the various combinations which have sought to lodge modern functions in buildings composed of ancient elements, developed and perfected for other objects, betray, in spite of all the skill that has been brought to bear upon them, their bastard origin. In literature the same struggle between the ancient form so dear to scholars and the modern thought which was outgrowing it was long and obstinate. In literature the battle has been won by the modern thought. The models of Greece are not less prized for this. We seek them diligently, we ponder them with delight and instruction. We assimilate all of their principles that is true and beautiful, and we learn of them to belong to our day and to our nation, as they to theirs.

In all structure that from its nature is purely scientific—in fortifications, in bridges, in shipbuilding—we have been emancipated from authority by the stern organic requirements of the works. The modern wants spurned the traditional formula in these structures, as the modern life outgrew the literary molds of Athens. In all these structures character has taken the place of dilettantism, and if we have yet to fight for sound doctrine in all structure, it is only because a doctrine which has possession must be expelled, inch by inch, however unsound its foundation.

The developments of structure in the animal kingdom are worthy of all our attention if we would arrive at sound principles in building. The most striking feature in the higher animal organizations is the adherence to one abstract type. The forms of the fish and the lizard, the shape of the horse, and the lion, and the camelopard, are so nearly framed after one type that the adherence thereto seems carried to the verge of risk. The next most striking feature is the modification of the parts, which, if contemplated independently of the exposure and functions whose demands are thus met, seems carried to the verge of caprice. I believe few persons not conversant with natural history ever looked through a collection of birds, or fish, or insects, without feeling that they were the result of Omnipotence at play for mere variety's sake.

If there be any principle of structure more plainly inculcated in the works of the Creator than all others, it is the principle of unflinching adaptation of forms to functions. I believe that colors also, so far as we have discovered their chemical causes and affinities, are not less organic in relation to the forms they invest than are those forms themselves.

If I find the length of the vertebrae of the neck in grazing quadrupeds increased, so as to bring the incisors to the grass; if I find the vertebrae shortened in beasts of prey, in order to enable the brute to bear away his victims; if I find the wading birds on stilts, the strictly aquatic birds with paddles; if, in pushing still further the investigation, I find color arrayed either for disguise or aggression, I feel justified in taking the ground that organization is the primal law of structure, and I suppose it, even where my imperfect light cannot trace it, unless embellishment can be demonstrated. Since the tints as well as the forms of plants and flowers are shown to have an organic significance and value, I take it for granted that tints have a like character in the mysteriously clouded and pearly shell, where they mock my ken. I cannot believe that the myriads are furnished, at the depths of the ocean, with the complicated glands and absorbents to nourish those dyes, in order that the hundreds may charm my idle eye as they are tossed in disorganized ruin upon the beach.

Let us dwell for a moment upon the forms of several of the higher types of animal structure. Behold the eagle as he sits on the lonely cliff, towering high in the air; carry in your mind the proportions and lines of the dove and mark how the finger of God has, by the mere variation of diameters, converted the type of meekness into the most expressive symbol of majesty. His eye, instead of rushing as it were out of his head, to see the danger behind him, looks steadfastly forward from its deep cavern, knowing no danger but that which it pilots. The structure of his brow allows him to fly upward with his eyes in shade. In his beak and his talons we see at once the belligerent, in the vast expanse of his sailing pinions the patent of his prerogative. *Dei Gratia Raptor!* Whence the beauty and majesty of the bird? It is the oneness of his function that gives him his grandeur, it is transcendental mechanism alone that begets his beauty. Observe the lion as he stands! Mark the ponderous predominance of his anterior extremities, his lithe loins, the lever of his hock, the awful breadth of his jaws, and the depth of his chest. His mane is a cuirass, and when the thunder of his voice is added to the glitter of his snarling jaws, man alone with all his means of defense stands self-possessed before him. In this structure again are beheld, as in that of the eagle, the most terrible expression of power and dominion, and we find that it is here also the result of transcendental mechanism. The form of the hare might well be the type of swiftness for him who never saw the greyhound. The greyhound overtakes him, and it is not possible in organization that this result should obtain, without the promise and announcement of it, in the lengths and diameters of this breed of dogs.

Let us now turn to the human frame, the most beautiful organization of earth, the exponent and minister of the highest being we immediately know. This stupendous form, towering as a lighthouse, commanding by its posture a wide horizon, standing in relation to the brutes where the spire stands in relation to the lowly colonnades of Greece and Egypt, touching earth with only one-half the soles of its feet—it tells of majesty and dominion by that upreared spine, of duty by those unencumbered hands. Where is the ornament of this frame? It is all beauty, its motion is grace, no combination of harmony ever equaled, for expression and variety, its poised and stately gait; its voice is music, no cunning mixture of wood and metal ever did more

than feebly imitate its tone of command or its warble
of love. The savage who envies or admires the special
attributes of beasts maims unconsciously his own perfection to assume their tints, their feathers, or their
claws; we turn from him with horror, and gaze with
joy on the naked Apollo.

I have dwelt a moment on these examples of expression and of beauty that I may draw from them a principle in art, a principle which, if it has been often
illustrated by brilliant results, we constantly see neglected, overlooked, forgotten—a principle which I hope
the examples I have given have prepared you to accept
at once and unhesitatingly. It is this: in art, as in nature, the soul, the purpose of a work will never fail to
be proclaimed in that work in proportion to the subordination of the parts to the whole, of the whole to the
function. If you will trace the ship through its various
stages of improvement, from the dugout canoe and the
old galley to the latest type of the sloop-of-war, you
will remark that every advance in performance has
been an advance in expression, in grace, in beauty, or
grandeur, according to the functions of the craft. This
artistic gain, effected by pure science in some respects,
in others by mere empirical watching of functions
where the elements of the structure were put to severe

tests, calls loudly upon the artist to keenly watch traditional dogmas and to see how far analogous rules may guide his own operations. You will remark, also, that after mechanical power had triumphed over the earlier obstacles, embellishment began to encumber and hamper ships, and that their actual approximation to beauty has been effected, first, by strict adaptation of forms to functions, second, by the gradual elimination of all that is irrelevant and impertinent. The old chairs were formidable by their weight, puzzled you by their carving, and often contained too much else to contain convenience and comfort. The most beautiful chairs invite you by a promise of ease, and they keep that promise; they bear neither flowers nor dragons, nor idle displays of the turner's caprice. By keeping within their province they are able to fill it well. Organization has a language of its own, and so expressive is that language that a makeshift or make-believe can scarce fail of detection. The swan, the goose, the duck, when they walk toward the water are awkward, when they hasten toward it are ludicrous. Their feet are paddles, and their legs are organized mainly to move those paddles in the water; they, therefore, paddle on land, or as we say, waddle. It is only when their breasts are launched into the pond that their necks assume the expression of ease and grace. A serpent upon a smooth hard road has a similar awkward expression of impotence; the grass, or pebbles, or water, as he meets either, afford him his *sine quâ non,* and he is instantly confident, alert, effective.

If I err not, we should learn from these and the like examples, which will meet us wherever we look for them, that God's world has a distinct formula for every function, and that we shall seek in vain to borrow shapes; we must make the shapes, and can only effect this by mastering the principles.

It is a confirmation of the doctrine of strict adaptation that I find in the purer Doric temple. The sculptures which adorned certain spaces in those temples had an organic relation to the functions of the edifice; they took possession of the worshiper as he approached, lifted him out of everyday life, and prepared him for the presence of the divinity within. The world has never seen plastic art developed so highly as by the men who translated into marble, in the tympanum and the metope, the theogony and the exploits of the heroes. Why, then, those columns uncarved? Why, then, those lines of cornice unbroken by foliages, unadorned by flowers? Why that matchless symmetry of every member, that music of gradation, without the tracery of the Gothic detail, without the endless caprices of arabesque? Because those sculptures *spake,* and speech asks a groundwork of silence and not of babble, though it were of green fields.

I am not about to deny the special beauties and value of any of the great types of building. Each has its meaning and expression. I am desirous now of analyzing that majestic and eloquent simplicity of the Greek temple, because, though I truly believe that it is hopeless to transplant its forms with any other result than an expression of impotent dilettantism, still I believe that its principles will be found to be those of all structures of the highest order.

When I gaze upon the stately and beautiful Parthenon, I do not wonder at the greediness of the moderns to appropriate it. I do wonder at the obtuseness which allowed them to persevere in trying to make it work in the towns. It seems like the enthusiasm of him who should squander much money to transfer an Arabian stallion from his desert home, that, as a blindfolded gelding, he might turn his mill. The lines in which Byron paints the fate of the butterfly that has fallen into the clutches of its childish admirer[1] would

---

[1] [In *The Giaour,* the passage (lines 388–421) including:
"For every touch that wooed its stay
Hath brushed its brightest hues away," etc.]

apply not inaptly to the Greek temple at the mercy of a sensible building committee, wisely determined to have their money's worth.

When high art declined, carving and embellishment invaded the simple organization. As the South Sea Islanders have added a variety to the human form by tattooing, so the cunning artisans of Greece undertook to go beyond perfection. Many rhetoricians and skilled grammarians refined upon the elements of the language of structure. They all spake: and demigods, and heroes, and the gods themselves, went away and were silent.

If we compare the simpler form of the Greek temple with the ornate and carved specimens which followed it, we shall be convinced, whatever the subtlety, however exquisite the taste that long presided over those refinements, that they were the beginning of the end, and that the turning-point was the first introduction of a fanciful, not demonstrable, embellishment, and for this simple reason, that, embellishment being arbitrary, there is no check upon it; you begin with acanthus leaves, but the appetite for sauces, or rather the need of them, increases as the palate gets jaded. You want jasper, and porphyry, and serpentine, and giallo antico, at last. Nay, you are tired of Aristides the Just, and of straight columns; they must be spiral, and by degrees you find yourself in the midst of a barbaric pomp whose means must be slavery—nothing less will supply its waste,—whose enjoyment is satiety, whose result is corruption.

It was a day of danger for the development of taste in this land, the day when Englishmen perceived that France was laying them under contribution by her artistic skill in manufacture. They organized reprisals upon ourselves, and, in lieu of truly artistic combinations, they have overwhelmed us with embellishment, arbitrary, capricious, setting at defiance all principle, meretricious dyes and tints, catchpenny novelties of form, steam-woven fineries and plastic ornaments, struck with the die or pressed into molds. In even an ordinary house we look around in vain for a quiet and sober resting-place for the eye; we see naught but flowers, flourishes—the renaissance of Louis Quatorze gingerbread embellishment. We seek in vain for aught else. Our own manufacturers have caught the furor, and our foundries pour forth a mass of ill-digested and crowded embellishment which one would suppose addressed to the sympathies of savages or of the colored population, if the utter absence of all else in the market were not too striking to allow such a conclusion.

I do not suppose it is possible to check such a tide as that which sets all this corruption toward our shores. I am aware of the economical sagacity of the English, and how fully they understand the market; but I hope that we are not so thoroughly asphyxiated by the atmosphere they have created as to follow their lead in our own creation of a higher order. I remark with joy that almost all the more important efforts of this land tend, with an instinct and a vigor born of the institutions, toward simple and effective organization; and they never fail whenever they toss overboard the English dictum and work from their own inspirations to surpass the British, and there, too, where the world thought them safe from competition.

I would fain beg any architect who allows fashion to invade the domain of principles to compare the American vehicles and ships with those of England, and he will see that the mechanics of the United States have already outstripped the artists, and have, by the results of their bold and unflinching adaptation, entered the true track, and hold up the light for all who operate for American wants, be they what they will.

In the American trotting wagon I see the old-fashioned and pompous coach dealt with as the old-fashioned palatial display must yet be dealt with in this land. In vain shall we endeavor to hug the associations connected with the old form. The redundant must be pared down, the superfluous dropped, the necessary itself reduced to its simplest expression, and then we shall find, whatever the organization may be, that beauty was waiting for us, though perhaps veiled, until our task was fully accomplished.

Far be it from me to pretend that the style pointed out by our mechanics is what is sometimes miscalled an economical, a cheap style. No! It is the dearest of all styles! It costs the thought of men, much, very much thought, untiring investigation, ceaseless experiment. Its simplicity is not the simplicity of emptiness or of poverty; its simplicity is that of justness, I had almost said, of justice. Your steam artisan would fill your town with crude plagiarisms, *calqués* upon the thefts from Pompeii or modern Venice, while the true student is determining the form and proportions of one article.

Far be it from me to promise any man that when he has perfected the type of any artistic product he shall reap the fruit of his labor in fame or money. He must not hope it. Fame and money are to be had in plenty; not in going against the current, but in going with it. It is not difficult to conceive that the same state of the popular taste which makes the corrupted style please will render the reformed style tasteless. It is not possible to put artistic products to a test analogous to that which tries the ship and the carriage but by a lapse of time. True it is that society always reserves a certain number of minds and of eyes unpoisoned by the vogue of the hour, and in the sympathy of these must the artist often find his chief reward in life.

Fashion in Relation to Progress

ASHION HAS LIVED TOO long, and exercised an influence too potent for us either to deny or to escape it. I wish to analyze it briefly. The fact that it runs counter to functional requirement oft-times, that it is imperative for its hour, and that it loses all claim even to respect or gratitude after that hour is passed, brings it into the same category with certain British sovereigns, who are stamped as the first gentle-men and ladies of Christendom as long as they sit upon the throne, and who are found, by subsequent analysis, to require a new definition of decency or propriety to bring them within the class of reputable men.

I regard the Fashion as the instinctive effort of the stationary to pass itself off for progress: its embellishment exhibits the rhythm of organization, without the capacity for action; so the Fashion boasts the sensuous phenomena of progress, without any real advance. The one and the other are, I believe, opiates, intended to quell and lull the wholesome demands of nature and of the author of nature. I believe both are better than nothing; for a false homage to the good has more of hope in it than a conscious and hearty adherence to wrong.

Wherever the student of modern life turns his eye, he sees, among other apparently more substantial and serious obstacles to advancement and reform, a phantom-like opponent who, though no man may say whence he comes, or who is his sire, assumes the purple and rules with a rod of iron. I mean the Fashion. I mean the essential *model* I do not mean to reflect upon the victims and subjects of this despot. I believe we all bow the neck to him, more or less; nor do I mean to assert that he has no right of any sort to our regard, for he has might, and might always means something very serious. I wish to put him to the test of analysis and find an intelligible definition of him, that I may know at least where and how far we may lazily submit, when and how we may rebel with a chance of freedom.

The Fashion is not coëval with the race—he was not a younger brother of the sun and stars, a second-born of Heaven. The great civilizations of antiquity never saw him till the epoch of their decline. The Iliad and the Greek tragedies have no trace of him. Even the modern man, in his hour of travail and of woe, wots not of him; he is a flutterer in the sunshine of superfluity. He is protean, elusive, he is here and gone; and when we had believed him dead, is here again in the twinkling of an eye! We had hoped that his change was a search after the good, until we felt that he gloried in the no-logic of his shifting. We had hoped that he was seeking a wise folly, and that when the circle of folly was run he would turn to wisdom in despair. But again and again he flies to the old folly and gilds with his sanction the exploded silliness of a few years since.

The Fashion is no respecter of persons. He has apparently no preferences of a distinct and reliable nature. He gives no premonitory symptoms of his approach. He expires in full vigor and, like Tadur, reappears in the form of some other impotent, dumb, and voiceless form.

His essential characteristic is change; he is a dodger, an ever new countersign, a Bramah lock,[1] which, when

---

[1] [The Bramah lock, named for its English inventor, was supposedly pick-proof. It required a special key, and 200 guineas was offered to anyone who, without a Bramah key, could open it. An American lock expert, A. C. Hobbs, succeeded—in fifty-one hours.]

Mr. Hobbs has made his key, instantly becomes a common padlock, and so puts him to shame.

I understand by the Fashion the instinctive effort of pretension to give by mere change the sensuous semblance of progress. I look upon it as a *pis aller* of the stationary to pass itself off for locomotion. I regard it as a uniform with which thinking humanity cripples its gait in the vain hope that the unthinking may keep up with itself. It is a result of the desperate effort to make a distinction out of nothing, and is only driven from change to change because nothing is a fruit that grows within the reach of all.

Still, Fashion denotes a hope of better things. It betrays a lurking want not clearly expressed, and it gives stones and serpents to stop our craving, only because it has neither bread nor fishes to bestow. Fashion is no positive evil, and has been often a relative good. As etiquette, though a poor makeshift, still confesses the existence of propriety, its superstition, with all its darkness, would prove a twilight to the godless; so Fashion may be allowed to protest against finality and be the symbol of yearning yet impotent aspiration.

Index